Masters of Peace

Masters of Peace is a book series edited by the University of Innsbruck's UNESCO Chair for Peace Studies. It has been founded to honour outstanding works of young academics in the field of Peace and Conflict Studies. It is reserved for selected Master theses of the Innsbruck school and published twice a year. The Innsbruck school follows the principles of Transrational Peace Philosophy. It defines peace as a plural and regards all aspects of human nature relevant for the understanding of peace and conflict. Its applied method is Elicitive Conflict Transformation, a pragmatic approach to conflict rooted in Humanistic Psychology that entrusts the responsibility for finding alternative options of behaviour, communication and encounter to the conflict parties. Facilitators provide a safe frame, tools and methods for this quest without imposing their own solutions on the parties.

Morten Frederiksen

Synchronicity as Transpersonal Modality

An Exploration of Jungian Spirituality in the Frame of Transrational Philosophy

Springer

Morten Frederiksen
Innsbruck, Austria

ISSN 2364-463X ISSN 2364-4648 (electronic)
Masters of Peace
ISBN 978-3-658-14227-8 ISBN 978-3-658-14228-5 (eBook)
DOI 10.1007/978-3-658-14228-5

Library of Congress Control Number: 2016939933

Springer

Printed on acid-free paper

This Springer imprint is published by Springer Nature
The registered company is Springer Fachmedien Wiesbaden GmbH

Table of Contents

1. Introduction

Γνῶθι σεαυτόν[1]

At the beginning of every academical text stands the personal question, why write, and on which topic? My general intention with the following work is to place myself within the transrational approach to peace-studies through processing the topic of *synchronicity* – a topic that has haunted me for many years now. Carl Rogers's insight that "the most personal also is the most universal," means by implication that the most universal also is the most personal. Consequently, it should indeed be possible to write something relevant for the general public by taking outset in a personal topic – and learn something deeply personal by engaging with universal topics and processes in a general way. This general statement of intent, which implies my plan to move between the only apparent poles of the personal and the universal in the widest sense, means particularly that by outlining phylogenetic and ontogenetic modes of consciousness and frames of reference in a transrational perspective, I expect to learn about and transform my personal mode of consciousness and understanding. By discussing the general findings in light of my personal interest in and experience of synchronicity, I hope on the other hand to be able to contribute to the transrational discourse on consciousness and frames of reference. As such, I understand this work as a dialog between the personal and the universal. Hence, in the following paragraph I will begin by grounding the topic in my own biography, and thus lay the ground for a subsequent research question and method.

[1] The Greek word *Γνῶθι σεαυτόν* (Gnōthi seautón – translated: Know Thyself) is not only the paradigmatic imperative for the elicitive conflict worker, but also the motto found at the gate of the Apollon temple in Delphi, known for its oracle (Tränkle 1985, 20).

1.1. Personal Perspective

In a certain sense, this work began in the summer of 2004 with my last summer-holidays, just turned eighteen and still at high school (Gymnasium). Two friends and I, tired of modern society, and philosophically connected to Thoreau and Rousseau´s motto "back to nature," took a car up to Sweden. We were searching for the deepest and most isolated forest, in order to live off the land for some weeks with no aids but our knives and axes. Since none of us had ever learned to live of the land, or even been serious boy-scouts – and since most forests we found were industrial pinewoods with ants as the seemingly only inhabitants - this endeavor became a mixed success. At some point, hungry, tired of my friends, and seriously craving some tobacco, we split up. I hitchhiked to Oslo, Norway, without any money, and without knowing anyone, with only dirty clothes in my backpack. I planned to make my way to Bergen, to visit a friend and lend some money for a ferry back to Kiel, close to Flensburg, Germany, where my home was. The rest of the holidays, where I never made it further than to Oslo and straight back to Flensburg (and back again to Oslo and again straight back to Flensburg), I deem worthy of a book by itself. However, the main lesson and experience on the way was how 'life' has a way to 'magically' provide when I surrender to it. The point here, though, is something I discovered just after arriving back home.

1.1.2. The first Symbol – A Path with A Heart

I discovered how my 'initiatory' travel (after all it were my last summer-holiday just turned eighteen, and thus of legal age) had taken the shape of a heart, when painted on a map. I saw how I would have completed a whole heart shape if I had made it to Bergen and back from there, and how I only had managed a half heart the way I actually traveled. This struck me quite heavily, remembering that my family middle name, which I never received, would have been *Hjertmand* (in English "heart-man") a circumstance I had not considered previously. This highly symbolic circumstance occupied my mind quite a lot (and was the reason for attempting to finish my heart-journey right away and hitchhike to Oslo twice). Symbolically, and fittingly enough, the first topic back at school in was the periods of Symbolism, with Henri-Frederic Amiel´s quote "Any landscape is a condition of the soul" as its motto (here quoted after Shanks 1924, 645). I remember thinking that the teacher and pupils got no clue what symbolism actually is about (and neither did I in retrospect). But from that time on my mind and senses were tuned in to see symbolic accordance and correspondences happen in my life and that of others - something that happened and happens all the time.

1.1.3. The Language of Life

From there it was not far to experience something I, in lack of other words, came to call "the language of life." While the symbolism with the heart on a map were quite abstract and only recognized in retrospect, this new form of experience happened right in the here and now, apparently speaking to me directly. What I experienced were symbolic happenings, often telepathically answering my very thoughts and feelings in the moment. These could be as everyday as the sound of an ambulance, or fireworks, or simple cheering somewhere, having a profound meaningful connection to my inner life. For instance, I could go to my kitchen in the morning, wondering whether I should let my cat climb on the roof (I was living on the 4th floor) and turning on the radio, the announcer would relate that cats are superb climbers, and often survive falls from as high as the 6th floor. Of course, when such things happen only occasionally, one, with my cultural background, takes it as stunning coincidence, as in random *chance*. However, if such coincidences keep accumulating, eventually the *chance* theory collapses. I got quite weary of ambulances and the radio at some point. Those symbolical incidences did not just relate to me but also relate to things and people happening around me. What I am talking about are incidents, for instance a near car-crash just outside our home, accompanied by heavy honking, just in the moment where the girlfriend of my flat mate was ringing the doorbell. If you now think that this probably was a rather bad omen, then you are in line with my reasoning. After she left, I learned from my flat mate that she just broke up with him. Following the proverb that "the teacher shows up when the student is ready," I came by 'chance' to read C. G. Jung´s (1964) book "Man and his Symbols," learning among other things that what I was experiencing is called *synchronicity*.

1.1.4. Messages from the Animal Kingdom

Inspired by Jung´s symbolism, I started to buy books about symbols in general, and 'power-animals' and 'animal-messengers' in particular. I learned about the symbolical meanings of the different animals, and experienced a profound change of perception – where often the smallest things were full of striking and intrinsic meaning, and my synchronistic experiences thus further increased dramatically. This is because, if you are not aware of the mythological and symbolical dimension of animals (and virtually all kind of entities around), you might walk or sit in a particular mood having corresponding thoughts and not realize how the dove landing before your feet symbolically reflects or meaningfully answers what is going inside yourself. In the following, I will give a personal and more recent example in this regard, which demonstrate the subtlety involved in synchronistic events.

In February 2014, while pondering the question whether to write on synchronicity or not, and being doubtful if there really is material for a serious thesis, or whether I am just 'too far out there' (and in a sense thus a victim of my own pipe dreams), I was walking to the local swimming bath in order to have a sauna. Actually, this happened two hours earlier than planned, since we would have visitors who changed their plans last minute, and so my mother, whom I was visiting, urged me to go earlier. As I was walking, suddenly a magpie jumped out quite close in front of me, making some strange twists and taking off *twice* before landing on the next tree. This behavior struck me as rather peculiar. I thought, if there really is something to synchronicity, and if micro-patterns indeed reflect bigger patterns in a meaningful and personal way, I should be able to read something from the behavior of this magpie. I thought that I was on my way to the sauna, which I wanted to attend repeatedly, and where the first sauna session is usually the most enjoyable. However, I figured since this magpie started off *twice* before actually getting somewhere, the second sauna session may hold something special in store for me. My interpretation of the magpie's behavior, and my expectations toward my *second* walk to the sauna struck me as strange, but I thought that maybe I would meet someone special or something like that. What happened? When I came to the bath hall, the waiter told me the sauna was closed and would open only *two* hours later – at *two* o´clock. If I wanted to have a sauna, I would indeed have to take a *second* walk, quite differently from how I had first figured! While I arguably was on a fitting track with my initial thinking, the incident - besides affirming synchronicity - also demonstrates the difficulty in interpreting such patterns correctly. That was the analogous side of the patterns. Some weeks later I happened to look into the book "Tierboten" by Angela Kämper, and read that according to her the spiritual (symbolical) message of the magpie is "unbelief." Kämper writes:

> The magpie wants with its appearance make obvious that you are torn back and forth between denying and accepting the spiritual dimension in the world generally – or maybe just in your own world. Probably you have had different extra-sensory perceptions or marvelous encounters. But your mind cannot comprehend those dimensions and for instance fobs you off with pseudo-scientific explanations (...) The bird invites you, to put more weight on your heart and inner voice. The bird brings you courage to believe what you sense with your subtle senses (...) you will realize that the contradiction between mind and intuition, science and faith and between chance and fate is not so irreconcilable, as you believe so far. (Kämper 2005, 267-268)

Another keyword in Kämper´s text regarding the magpie was "confusion" (Ibid.). While the magpie thus quite profoundly reflected and spoke to to my inner situation in this particular moment, a crucial characteristic of such a synchronicity is that for a moment there is a profound confluence between the inner intent or meaning of the observer, and the outer manifestations – in other words the observer and the observed are in a meaningful way one. Such coincidences are in the 'normal' Western frame of reference interpreted as likely stunning, but at heart random chance happenings, without a meaningful underlying dynamic, or simply treated as the constructions of a schizophrenic mind. If, however, such incidents begin to accumulate, as they normally do once one starts to look for them, however subtle, eventually the chance theory collapses, and other interpretations are needed. Jung points towards this:

> Since archetypal situations are not uncommon in schizophrenia, we must also suppose that corresponding synchronistic phenomena will occur which follow exactly the same course as with so -called normal persons. The difference lies simply and solely in the interpretation. The schizophrenic´s interpretation is morbidly narrow because it is mostly restricted to the intentions of other people and to his own ego-importance. The normal interpretation ... is based on the philosophic premise of the symphathy of all things, or something of that kind ... If synchronicities occur in these cases it is because an archetypal situation is present, for whenever archetypes are constellated we find manifestations of the primordial unity. Thus the synchronistic effect should be understood not as a psychotic but as a normal phenomenon. (Adler and Jaffé 1975, 409).

What Jung does not mention is that schizophrenic minds indeed are more likely to see synchronistic effects due to their typical high emotional charge, something Jung ascribes to the constellation of an archetype, and in turn connects to synchronistic events, which, due to their egocentric frame of reference that more often than not relates everything to the ego, and thus is prone to see such relations, however distorted. Otherwise I can retrospectively only agree with Jung, since "the sympathy of all things." and equally pantheistic interpretations also were the way I conceptualized my own private observations – *notabene* before ever reading Jung. I do thus also completely agree with Marie-Louise von Franz:

> The most essential and certainly the most impressive thing about synchronistic occurrences (...) is the fact that in them the duality of soul and matter seems eliminated. They are therefore an *empirical* indication of an ultimate unity of all existence, which Jung, using the terminology of medieval natural philosophy, called the *unus mundus* (Franz, 1975, 247).

This *unus mundus*, this "ultimate unity of all existence," in which Von Franz sees *synchronistic occurences* an indication, reminds and leads the associations towards the transrational notion of the All-One, and means the same thing. The Jungian psychologist Jean Shinoda Bolen poignantly states that "the value of synchronicity lies in its ability to connect us to a meaning-giving, intuitively known principle in our lives by which we can find a "path with heart," a *tao*, a way to live in harmony with the universe" (Bolen 2004, xiv). This is arguably another description of the transrational peace-effort. Bolen further states that at the most profound level, synchronicity can lead us to the awareness that we are part of something far greater than ourselves, and to a sense of wholeness in the archetype of the Self, metaphorically expressed by the Grail Legend, by the concept of the Kingdom of God, or by returning to the Tao (Ibid., xv). The psychologist C. T. Frey-Wehrlin goes in the same direction:

> It seems to me that the principle of synchronicity, as introduced by Jung, could prove as decisive for psychology as the quantum theory proved for physics, and as revolutionary, inasmuch it compels us to re-think our premises (Frey-Wehrlin 1976, 39).

The premises Frey-Wehrlin has in mind are the duality of mind and matter, the atomized Newtonian, modern and mechanistic worldview, from which Quantum Physics literally has pulled the rug out under its feet. Synchronicity likewise points to a reality unbound by space and time – a primordial unity of existence, similar to the transrational notion of the All-One.

I believe it is no exaggeration to state that the transrational All-One as both experienceable reality and theoretical formulation is the goal and basis for transrational peace-efforts. As the ultimate accordance of peace and imaginable state of consciousness, it is the goal of peace-oriented psychological development. As ultimate reality it is the basis for peace-oriented, transrational theory building. If we are all one, then the ethical *golden rule* - do unto others as you wish to be treated yourself – and the Kantian categorical imperative are transformed into absolute Imperatives, not only grounded in metaphysical reason and humanistic idea(l)s about justice, contestable by utilitarian counter-concepts, but grounded in a reality, where treating the other really means to treat oneself – where there is no 'I,' 'we' and 'other' - but finally only all. The All-One is furthermore the basis for the tantric principle of correspondence, from which transrational methodology and practice derive. As such it is safe to say that every inquiry into and elaboration on the All-One is of highest relevance for peace-studies.

With these few introductory remarks, I hope to have established from the bottom up the relevance of - and the seemingly connection between – synchronicity and the All-One. The arguably well-founded hunch that there exists a connection between those two topics constitutes the greater point of departure and hypothesis for my further inquiry. This is relevant for peace-studies, since if Jung is right in suggesting synchronicities as manifestations of the primordial unity, then Bolen could be equally correct stating that synchronicities constitute a mean to live in harmony with the universe - because they then could constitute communications with the wider mind(s)/All-One. Exactly how I wish to inquire into this relationship, and what questions I ask for which reasons, is the topic of the next paragraph.

1.2. Research Question

For above reasons, my initial interest is to understand synchronicity from a transrational perspective and investigate if, or how, a regard for synchronicities can be used in relation to the transpersonal All-One and an elicitive approach to conflict transformation. My initial question, and the springboard for this thesis, derived from above considerations is thus, *how can synchronicity be understood in a transrational perspective - and how does synchronicity relate to the transpersonality of the All--One?* Especially interesting here I find the question, in how far synchronicity might be the *medium* through which transpersonality and finally the All-One manifests itself? For anticipating some terms; can the dissolution of the perspective in the Witness awareness – the paradoxical flowing into each other of the intra-personal and the inter-personal layers, through which observer and observed are one – be described as synchronistic? Formulated differently; is the oneness of observer and observed in the Witness awareness a synchronistic reflection/relation? What on a first glance might look like asking strange questions with simple "yes or no" answers, could as a later consequence eventually prove to explain the trans-personal effects on which elicitive conflict transformation finally relies. To use another insider: in the end I will be able to explain not only *how* the Taoist rainmaker works – something that as description exists, but also *why* it actually rains – an explanation so far lacking in the discourse. First of all, however, my intention is to classify synchronicity within a transrational perspective.

1.3. Method

In order to answer the basic questions, I need on the one hand to explain synchronicity – and on the other hand to paint the contours of a transrational frame of reference to hold it up against. In this regard I have several theoretical and methodological options. Since the synchronicity-hypothesis is developed by Jung and closely connected to his whole psychology, I will outline and treat synchronicity from a Jungian perspective. This should be compatible with a transrational frame of reference, since Jung is held as forerunner for trans-personal psychology, which again is a cornerstone for transrational considerations. The Jungian approach to synchonicity is also compatible with my interest in synchronicity as 'inner' experience – that is, as a subjective mode of understanding, or reference, and what that means for the individual – and not so much whether synchronicity is an objective phenomena and what that says about the world we live in. As such I in many ways take outset in what Dietrich in reference to Ken Wilber calls the *inner-singular quadrant,* and the *inner-plural quadrant,* where he refers to this scientifically difficult to grasp inner world of human beings (Cf. Dietrich 2008, 385-388). What I then need is a transrational and psychological frame of reference that relates to the inner experiences and different cosmologies of human beings. As an Innsbruck peace-student who wishes to develop and work with the Innsbruckian discourse, I have two main theoretical outlines to work with in this regard. For one there is the historically oriented review and analysis of Wolfgang Dietrich concerning the so-called energetic, moral, modern, post-modern and transrational peaces as outlined in Dietrich (2008). This theoretical frame would already prove to be very convenient for my purpose, since the different categories also constitute different and generalized modes of consciousness, frames of reference and cosmologies, where it would be easy to demonstrate how synchronicity played a central part in energetic communities – especially in form of divination – and since the link between the energetic and the transrational also already is established, it would be easy to argue how a transrational epistemology also should regard synchronicity. However, this would say little about the *meaning* for the individual *persona,* and how synchronicities relate to the *persona* - and the *personal* via synchronicity to the All-One/Universal. For this I need the second theoretical tool, which is Dietrich´s diagram of *transrational peaces,* and constitutes an extension of Lederach´s conflict pyramid in consolidation with yogic chakra-psychology and Wilber´s transrational matrix. The diagram shows, among other things, the intra- and inter-personal layers of the *persona* outlined in reference to Ken Wilber coupled with an interpretation of chakra psychology following Shankya Yoga in the tradition of Patanjali, where every intra-personal layer corresponds to an inter-personal layer, built around the seven chakras (Dietrich 2014, 50).

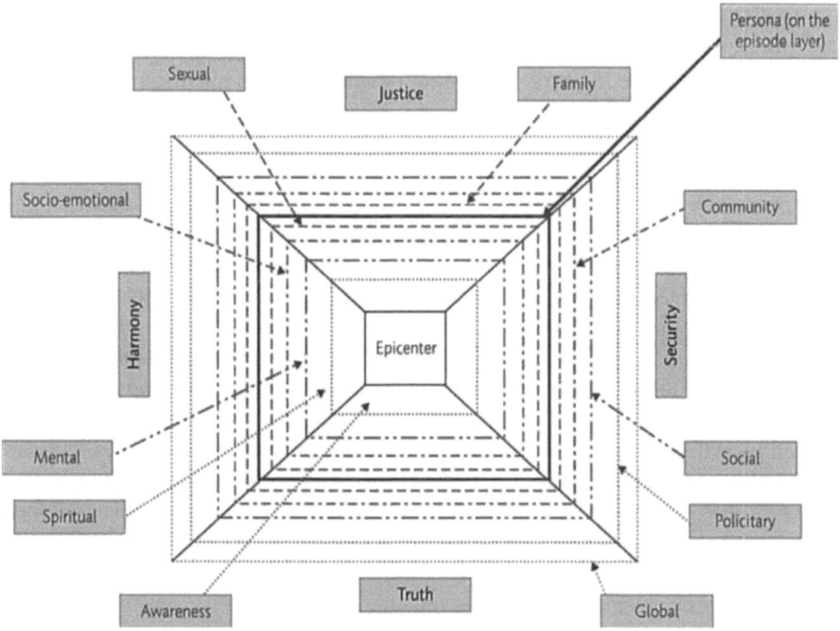

Figure 1. The diagram of Transrational Peace, bird's-eye view (First published in Dietrich, 2011, 357).

The four sides of the diagram are in correspondence with Wilber´s four quadrants, and correspond further to the five peace-families, where *energetic* corresponds to peace out of harmony, *moral* to peace out of justice, *modern* to peace out of security, and *post-modern* to peace out of truth. A regard for all sides in themselves and their depth then constitutes the *transrational*. The diagram shows the active, albeit not necessarily all consciously accessed layers constituting a normally and contemporary mature *persona*. For my purposes I will convert the different intra-personal layers to stages of consciousness in a psychological scheme. In order to do this, I will firstly draw on classical development psychology, according to which every person from birth onwards holds most of the layers as latent potential, but also gradually accesses, integrates and transcends the different layers, beginning from the physical border on the surface of the episode unto the mental layer, which corresponds to the social/societal layer and is where classical psychology ends. The spiritual layers unto the epicenter with the corresponding inter-personal layers, is then the area of transpersonal psychology. The by Dietrich applied tantric 'Principle of Correspondence,' which states “as above so below” and “as within so without”, might not only apply in the Moment, but also over time, because many scholars see empirical evidence suggesting a profound correlation – or correspondence – between ontogenetic and phylogenetic development. This means that these theorists suggest that not only does every human in its individual development go through the same stages, but humankind has done and does so as well[2]. The transrational school around Dietrich rejects evolutionary oriented developmental interpretations of psychological growth, and especially ontogenetic and phylogenetic parallelism on several grounds; of which the tendentious and historically evident violence against what is perceived as less developed and the anachronistic teleological implications of such a reading are the most prominent (Cf. Dietrich 2008, 105; Dietrich 2015, 23). Dietrich differentiates in this regard between the *human growth* and the *human potential* movements, which are often mixed up and unfortunately used interchangeable. Roughly put, *human growth* denotes an understanding of every human taking part in a collective, teleological guided growth-process, which through a series of developmental stages in a sort of Hegelian dialectic reaches ever higher spheres of consciousness, while *human potential* denotes the understanding that every human from birth on is equipped with a species specific consciousness-potential, which biographically conditioned is more or less actualized (Dietrich 2015, 20). I agree with Dietrich´s criticism of the *human growth* movement, which with its promise of final salvation continues in the logic of the liberal belief in progress, historical materialism, fascism, and the modern idealistic belief in development, and thus is old wine in new wineskins and subject to the same pitfalls these schools have and do face (Ibid. 21). I further agree with the assessment of the *human potential* movement and the transrational school in that the described layers at least latently exist, and potentially are accessible for every human and have been since the brain of *homo sapiens* stopped to mutate an estimated 200.000 years ago, while what the single human actually is experiencing has everything to do with its biography and the social, emotional, and physical surroundings it is embedded in – and not a chronological, teleological guided civilizing progress.

However, this does not mean that a transrational oriented approach, or the *human potential movement* for that sake, rejects the findings of classical development psychology or anthropological findings concerning different people's different cosmologies – and correlations between these cosmologies and their societal organization. When I in the following thus nevertheless draw on the material of Habermas and Wilber regarding ontogenetic and phylogenetic parallels, it is because I believe their material contains valuable insights into the different layers as described by Dietrich, without thereby having to import their evolutionary and teleological interpretations as well. During my research for this work, I have indeed come to the conclusion that it is possible to correlate

[2] Paradigmatic in this regard are Habermas (1979) and Wilber (2000).

ontogenetic development stages to the four first chakras and layers of the diagram of Transrational Peace. Additionally, I believe that the evidence which theorists like Gebser, Habermas and Wilber present towards a further correlation of these layers to existing cosmovisions and frames of reference among historic and contemporary cultures and people, simply is too compelling to be ignored. Just as the diagram of Transrational Peace correlates intra-personal structures to inter-personal structures and holds an epicenter which is synonymous with peace-as-such, without thereby implying any teleology or value-judgement in regard to those layers, I will in the following demonstrate the possibility to further correlate ontogenetic stages and phylogenetic variations to those layers, without implying teleological assumptions or making value-judgements. While this might be a daring endeavor where I easily could slip off into contradictions and be misread as holding an evolutionist agenda, I believe it is not more risky in this regard than formulating a pyramid where the top is the ultimate experience of peace, while the building as such consists of blocks and material imported from a tradition, where the same material for instance has constructed a cast system. "Prove all things; hold fast that which is good" shall also be my motto here.

While the intellectual dangers in sipping from the forbidden juice of ontogenetic and phylogenetic parallelism are great, the benefits when done carefully are equally great. The advantage of aligning forms of societal organization and their corresponding cosmologies with individual states of consciousness is a considerably broader and deeper understanding of these different layers and stages. With this approach I can thus deepen the understanding of the transrational diagram, but also expose weaknesses. For instance, it will become evident that *harmony*, which corresponds to the *energetic,* also corresponds to the first three chakras, while *justice* and *security* correspond to the fourth (and maybe fifth) chakra, and while *truth* relates to the last chakras. As such the four sides of the pyramid in some sense become obsolete, because their meaning-content already shows to be represented in the different layers[3].

Such an approach could be a starting point for re-classifying and for further differentiation of the different peace-families – where I (following every structure/chakra) would end up with seven families instead of the five described by Dietrich. This, however, is only a 'side-effect' of my outline, while my main goal is to develop a (transrational) model, which takes outset in, and describes different forms of consciousness in relation to the existing model. Once this is

---

[3] Since the pyramid form-wise seems more related to the mental layer symbolizing a hierarchical perspective, a three-dimensional moving globe could be a fitting alternative frame and symbol for a transrational tool, in line with Gebser's proposal for his integral structure (Cf. Gebser 1973, 175-176).

done, it will be possible to take Jung´s psychology and especially the concept of synchronicity and compare it to the developed model – and hence understand synchronicity in a transrational terminology. I expect to find Jung´s individuation process compatible with the diagram of Transrational Peace and being able to decide in how far the synchronistic logic constitutes a regress to pre-modern irrationality or has to do with transpersonality. I further expect that my findings may not be an 'either or' answer, but rather that synchronicities might both explain and account for much of *energetic* spirituality as well as *transpersonality* – while the difference simply might be between conscious aspiration and intuitive doing. The key to understanding synchronicity I believe at this point lies in emotional *energy* and *feelings* and how they process space and time transcending in the world expressing themselves symbolically. Since feelings and emotions are quite fundamental, in the sense that they are close to the archaic origin of the psyche, and synchronicities also are a "medium" of transpersonality, studying synchronicity in this frame I expect to gain new insights into the relationship between pre-modern spirituality and transpersonal modalities of peace.

1.4. State of the Art

The following survey of academical literature and the state of the art within the academical debate and research is divided in two parts, according to the two main areas of interest of this paper. This is namely Jungian psychology and synchronicity on the one hand, and transrational peace-philosophy and consciousness development on the other.

1.4.1. The Synchronicity Debate

Carl Gustav Jung´s basic treatise on synchronicity, called "Synchronizität als ein Prinzip akausaler Zusammenhänge" [1952], together with the statements on synchronicity contained in his foreword to the Wilhelm-Baynes version of the *I Ching* (1950) are the only two texts where Jung addressed and coined the term (and problem) of synchronicity directly. Unfortunately, Jung in his main work does not outline how the concept of synchronicity relates to his psychology as a whole, but uses most of his energy to defend and guard the existence of synchronicity against expected ridicule from the wider academic community by discussing statistic probabilities, modern ontological assumptions, and by comparing the synchronicity-concept to older philosophical concepts – here especially Leibniz' Monadology, Taoist philosophy, and diverse alchemical and Medieval texts. He accomplishes to make a strong argument for the reality of the existence of *meaningful connections* of some otherwise seemingly unrelated coincidences – contrary to a *pure chance* or constructivist explanation. Based on Jung´s work, I take the reality of synchronistic connections as given, and refer the reader to the mentioned Jung literature regarding an argument in this direction. In order to understand Jung´s point of view within his own context, I find his later works especially helpful. An easily accessible introduction to Jungian psychology constitutes the already mentioned book "Man and his Symbols" (Jung 1964), as well as Jolande Jacobi´s (1978) "Die Psychologie von C. G. Jung", while especially "On The Nature of the Psyche" (Jung 1969) in many ways constitutes Jung´s final words on his psychology. While following up on cross-references I am in my thesis in the end drawing on Jung´s complete work as published in the "Collective Works".

It comes as no surprise that most scholars who write on synchronicity are analytical psychologists – and given the Jung-Pauli connection – physicians with an interest in psychology. Almost all contemporary scholars who write on synchronicity invariably take outset in Jung´s initial comments, either producing a slight variation combined and reinterpreted with new inputs - or discussing what Jung might have meant in the first place[4]. A reason for this is surely that Jung´s formulations never reached a concluding stage. Among Jung´s immediate followers, Marie-Louise von Franz wrote most extensively on synchronicity in "Number and Time" (1974), and the published lecture series "On Divination and Synchronicity: The Psychology of Meaningful Chance Studies in Jungian Psychology" (1980), where she is taking up hints from Jung´s original text concerning the relation between synchronicity and natural numbers. This has led her into explorations concerning the emerging interface between physics and psychology, and towards some suggestive speculations concerning the working of divinatory processes such as the I Ching. I refer to her work throughout my work where it seems relevant. However, her work is mostly concerned with ontological questions based on a rather unique form of "numerology," while I am more concerned with the implications for transrational peace-studies.

Perhaps the best and most illuminating work within the Jungian psychological field, and highly contributive for my own understanding of the phenomena in question was the book "C. G. Jung´s Psychology of Religion and Synchronicity" (1990) by Robert Atziz. The author masterfully incorporates the synchronicity-concept into the Jungian psychology as a whole with a special focus on Jung´s

[4] See for instance Wolfgang Giegerich (2012), where the author argues that many scholars misunderstand synchronicity due to the circumstance that they do not read Jung in the original German version, but in an English translation. The author, himself Jungian analyst, is clearly not willing to accept the slightest consequences of Jung´s formulations.

psychology of religion, in other words the famous individuation-process. He argues why and how synchronistic occurrences form part of the general compensatory activity of the unconscious – something Jung never made explicit, but is a logic consequence of Jung´s thoughts. He further points out, demonstrating a comprehensive knowledge of Jung´s work and personal life, how Jung´s personal life and work as an analyst was much more guided by his experiences and recognition of synchronicity as hints from 'higher' (or deeper) ordering and intelligent powers, than his texts may indicate.

In the same direction as Atziz argues Victor Mansfield, a contemporary physician and Jungian trained analyst, who also interprets synchronicity as a compensatory activity within the context of individuation in his book "Synchronicity, Science and Soul Making" (1995). He was helpful for me in demarcating synchronicity against ESP and other paranormal phenomena, as he is reserving the term synchronicity solely for the compensatory activity of the Self, while his main focus is on quantum physics and its correlation with middle way-buddhism, reminiscent of the work done by Fritjof Capra.

Another Jungian influenced line of approach to the understanding of synchronicity is the attempt to view the phenomena mythological in terms of which 'god' or 'spirit' might be responsible for synchronicities. Thus, a few authors have tried to elucidate aspects of synchronicity imaginatively or 'imagically,' viewing synchronicity as the expression of certain Greek gods: Hermes the trickster and transgressor of boundaries; Pan the god of spontaneity; or Dionysus, bestower of the experience of mystical fusion and timelessness[5]. The observation in regard to the trickster here is that many coincidences seem to make fun of the subjective experiencer, and the circumstance that meaningful coincidences are quite 'close' to everyday life, has led them to be associated with Hermes, the boundary dweller and "friendliest of the gods to man" (Kerenyi 1976, 104). Similarly, due to how inert matter can appear animated in synchronistic events has caused the phenomenon to be imaginatively explored in relation to the figure of the Golem (Mindell 1975).

There have also been more clinical emphasis within the Jungian contributions[6] besides numerous studies attempting to modify Jung´s theories[7], and relating synchronicity to, for instance, apparitions, the theories of relativity and quantum physics, and hypnotic induction[8]. The work of Roderick Main deserves an

[5] For Hermes, see Combs and Holland (1990). The authors also refer to trickster gods from other cultures, such as Ictinike, Coyote, Rabbit, and others from Native American mythology; Maui of the Polynesian Islanders; Loki of the old Germanic tribes of Europe; and Krishna from India (ibid., 82). For Pan, see Hillman (1972), for Dionysus, see Burniston (1994).

[6] For instance, see Fordham (1957; 1962) and Williams (1957).

[7] For instance, see Progoff (1973).

[8] For apparitions see Aniela Jaffé (1978), regarding relativity Gammon (1973), see Carolin S. Keutzer (1984) for a good article on quantum mechanics and Sandra Brenneis and Frederic Boersma (1993) for a speculative relation between synchronicity and hypnotic induction.

explicit mention, as he has demonstrated a keen insight into the subject, and in a recent study suggested synchronicity as spiritual experience (Main 2007). Finally, there has also been noteworthy research by Joseph Cambray attempting to relate synchronicity to processes of emergence and selforganization, arguing that synchronicity is a systemic-feature happening when new systems emerge (Cambray 2009).

Outside Jungian circles it was especially the novelist Arthur Koestler´s (1972) book "The roots of Coincidence" which introduced and made the term socially acceptable – or at least put it on a wider agenda. He accumulated a large collection of case material through public appeals in the media, while his reasoning on the subject besides a parapsychological perspective was greatly influenced by physics and the other hard sciences. Koestler assumed that there must be two complementary principles operating at all levels of reality; a self-assertive tendency, which enables entities to assert their individuality and autonomy, and an integrative tendency, by which those same entities remain subordinate to the larger whole of which they form part (Koestler 1972, 111-113). His explanation of coincidences is to see them as expressions of this integrative tendency, which he thought could be regarded as a universal principle, which includes a-causal phenomena (Ibid. 122). As such he is close to the transrational perspective developed in this paper.

Other authors have addressed the problem of coincidence from the perspectives of statistics and cognitive psychology. For instance, George Spencer Brown has argued that the apparent significance of coincidences may be due to a mistaken understanding of how statistics operate (Brown 1957, 154-156). Persi Diaconis and Frederick Mosteller, two mathematicans, have suggested that statistical considerations alone are able to explain away the apparent meaningfulness of most coincidences (Diaconis and Mosteller 1989). In response has it been noted that most real-life coincidences are so complex and diverse in its variables, that every attempt to fathom them statistically becomes dubious (Inglis 1990, 98-99). As also argued above, both Jung and von Franz question whether it is sensitive to apply statistics to synchronicity at all, since the former looks for the average by ignoring what is unique, while the latter exactly tries to investigate that uniqueness (Jung 1950; Franz 1980).

In the line of statistical reasoning Caroline Watt has summarized various considerations from a cognitive psychological perspective, which demonstrate that people normally are very poor judges of probability under the kind of uncertainty under which most meaningful coincidences take place, and are prone to process information erroneously. However, she notes that these considerations cut both ways, and could equally explain why certain events are judged to be normal, when in fact they are anomalous (Watt 1991, 82).

The only author who simultaneously denies the Jungian model, and applies cognitive psychology without trying to disprove synchronicity as meaningful coincidence, is the transpersonal psychologist Kirby Surprise. With his recent and rather popular scientific book "Synchronicity: The Art of Coincidence, Choice and unlocking your Mind" (2012) he has contributed a unique, trans-disciplinary perspective on the problem of synchronicity, which has to be taken seriously as the author reveals the most encompassing personal and intimate experience of synchronicities I have come across in the literature – besides Jung himself. While Koestler and Jung are exponents of different forms of holistic and transpersonal modalities held responsible for meaningful coincidences, Surprise occupies the opposite stance when he interprets synchronicities as outer reflections of inner states and thought patterns, and in the end thus holds the individual responsible for causing its own synchronicities. Rejecting Jung´s medieval analogies of micro-macrocosmic correspondence and sympathies, as well as universal All-One notions and trying just as hard to avoid archaic magical causality, he does not come around to apply quantum-physics and ancient anthropological analogies in order to explain the phenomena. The difference lies in the interpretation; while Jungian followers tend to a "hidden variables" interpretation of quantum-physics, and lately to Bohm´s holistic implicit/explicit order model, Surprise follows string-theoretical considerations. He argues that the postulated multidimensional M and N-fields of string-theory could hold the space-time transcending astral- and mental-bodies, which he considers responsible for the apparent space-time bending in instances of synchronicity (Surprise 2012, 237 - 245), and as concepts date back to at least the platonic and neoplatonic worldview, and also are found in the worldview of a Paracelsus and Agrippa von Nettesheim, and more recently among theosophists and for instance occultists as Franz Bardon (Bardon 1982).

With the mentioning above of the physicist David Bohm, the last promising area that has to be mentioned in relation to synchronicity is reached. Several authors have suggested that certain alternative scientific theories with an emphasis on holism may be relevant to an understanding of synchronicity[9]. As Roderick Main also points out, especially the centrality and flexibility of the information concept within both Bohm´s theory of the implicate order and Sheldrake's hypothesis of formative causation are very suggestive[10] (Main 2007, 8). The physician and assistant of David Bohm, Francis David Peat, approaches the topic of synchronicity in a well-founded science oriented fashion, when he tries to align the Jungian archetypes with the implicit order theory of Bohm, and explains synchronicity as particular instances in a general sort of creative feedback-loop between different layers of reality – and along the way suggests

[9] See for example, Combs and Holland (1996; 15, 18); Inglis (1990; 178 - 185) and F. David Peat (1989). The principal authors referred to by these writers are David Bohm (1980) and Rupert Sheldrake (1981; 1988).

[10] The concept of information also plays a role in Marie-Louise von Franz hypothetical connection between synchronicity and whole numbers (Von Franz 1974, 209-211), and Robert Robinson´s approach to the possible modus operandi of synchronicity (Robertson 2002, 108).

that the unique and numinous quality of synchronistic events mostly is due to erroneous pre-conceptions about the inner cohesion of reality (Peat 1989).

Sheldrake's contested hypothesis of formative causation proposes that the characteristic organization of systems depends on influences that lead to a repetition of specific forms and patterns of previous systems - by which laws of nature are no longer to be understood as strict laws, but rather as space and time transcending *habits* of nature, working by something called morphic resonance. Morphic resonance gives cohesion to morphogenetic fields, which again are proposed connected by the same quantum fields the science-future- and peace-researcher Ervin Laszlo invokes for his hypothetical Akasha-Field (Laszlo 2000). The hypothetical working of those fields holds potential explanatory power for synchronistic occurrences and the All-One[11]. However, since I am not so much concerned about the "technical" side of how synchronicity works, but more with its *meaning* for the individual within a transrational peace-psychological paradigm, this side of the topic will not concern me in the following.

1.4.2. Transrational Peace-Studies

This paper and my theoretical perspective takes outset, and is situated, in the Innsbruckian transrational peace-philosophy, which in terms of literature is outlined in the three volumes "Variationen über die vielen Frieden" by Prof. Wolfgang Dietrich (2008, 2011, 2015)[12]. Especially relevant for my thesis are the last chapters in the first two volumes, and the first chapter in the third volume, where Dietrich develops the diagram of transrational peace; in the first volume with a focus on the "construction plan" of the intra-personal layers of the *persona,* and in the second volume in relation to peace-work and the inter-personal layers (Ibid.).

Running parallel to Dietrich´s work and important for my own work as well is Ken Wilber´s "Sex, Ecology & Spirituality" (2000), where Wilber outlines an equal 'construction plan' of the psychological person and discusses the relation between inter- and intra-personal modalities. The evolutionist Wilber works as well on correspondences between ontogenetic and phylogenetic consciousness development, and is also in this sense fundamental for my own work. In this regard both Wilber and I draw on Jürgen Habermas text "Communication and

---

[11] Caroline S. Keutzer argues for instance in an article that Sheldrake's morphogenetic fields are theoretically highly compatible with the Jungian archetypes (Keutzer, 1982).

[12] I do also draw on the English translation of the first volume, "Interpretations of Peace in History and Culture" (Dietrich 2012).

the evolution of Society" (1979), where Habermas, aiming at a historical reconstruction of societal organization in relation to ego-formation and communication, concludes the work done in respect to phylo- and ontogenetic parallelism so far, and arguably sets the state of the art in this particular debate. Unlike Habermas and Wilber, I do not reduce the phylogenetic development to its ontogenetic correspondence. In other words, I do not believe that the neolithic human run around with the intelligence of a contemporary five-year old. I understand the parallels as symbolical correspondences equal to synchronistic reflections and driven by the same inner logic as synchronicities – and not as literal homologous correlation. When it comes to understanding the phylogenetic development of consciousness, for instance the archaic humans point of view, I have found no better than Jean Gebser and his work "Ursprung und Gegenwart" (1973), which still is ground-breaking in this regard, and is referred to throughout my work. Wilber shares my opinion about Gebser, however, our readings of Gebser differ substantially. Otherwise I draw on anthropological monographs, as far as such material is applicable. On this account Lucien Levy-Bruhl (Levy-Bruhl 1923) deserves mentioning, who not only wrote extensively on what back then without being politically incorrect was called 'primitive mentality,' but also coined the term *participation mystique*; a concept Jung borrowed, and which will be discussed in the context of understanding synchronicity as psychological phenomena.

With Jung I am already concerned with one of the trailblazers for humanistic and transpersonal psychology, which is one of the pillars on which the transrational discipline rests. In structuralistic terms, I could say that characteristic for humanistic and transpersonal psychological approaches is that they, compared to more modern mechanistic and especially post-freudian approaches, not only treat 'downwards,' which means to assume some form of normal functioning state of being, and everything diverging from this norm is treated as dysfunctional in need for treatment in order to gain a normal functioning state. They are also open 'upwards' towards tendentiously more positive states than the stalemate battlefield between the antagonistic libido and social necessities, which the Freudian ego constitutes. Paradigmatic here is Maslow´s hierarchy of needs, but also Jung´s individuation-process. In equally structuralistic peace-terminology this is comparable to Johan Galtung´s notion of positive and negative peace, where the former describes the simultaneous presence of many desirable states of mind and society, such as harmony, justice, equity, etc., while negative peace commonly denotes the absence of war or overt violence (Barash and Webel 2009, 4). Seldom added then is what exactly harmony, justice and equity should be, while the existing divergence in definitions historically has caused much violence. The question "what means are allowed to gain this justice, harmony, etc.?" is also seldom answered. Humanistic and later transpersonal psychology would here correspond to a work towards positive peace, contrary to a sole engagement with negative peace.

However, such a dialectical display of the psychological 'division of labor' has correspondingly a limited applicable, since both sides also are encompassing and are mutually exclusive wholes in themselves. For instance transpersonal psychologists tend to praise a Siberian shamans soul-journey as a desirable altered-state-of-consciousness including an out-of-body-experience, noting that it constitutes an expansion and thus a more full drawing of the human potential compared to an everyday state of consciousness, not mentioning the potential healing effect of the shamans work, while Freudians would tend to diagnose the same phenomena as hallucinatory, psychotic regress (Walsh 1993, 39-41). On the other hand, a by Freudians correctly diagnosed serious pathology on the verge of psychotic breakdown could by transpersonal psychologists be just as correctly interpreted as transpersonal crisis or initiatory sickness on the way to become a shaman or healer - addressed as the *wounded healer* phenomena (Hofmann and Roesler 2010, 76). Accordingly much focus in transpersonal psychology is directed towards differentiating between serious pathology and transpersonal crisis, and their mutual relation (Vaughan and Walsh 1993, 132). This distinction is also important for synchronicity, since also here the question arises whether some cases constitute self-referential thoughts or rather an experience of transpersonal dimensions. A prominent theoretical grit to examine this question, which also here will be applied, is Ken Wilber's pre/trans fallacy as outlined in "Sex, Ecology, & Spirituality" (Wilber 2000).

With the critique of modern psychology and the simultaneous application of for instance shamanic and age-old meditative techniques, transpersonal psychology practically re-integrates pre-modern and un-modern systems into a (post) modern context. That fact that transpersonal psychology from the outset is modern is already revealed by the term 'trans.' One can only consciously overstep or widen something (trans-cend) by a prior acknowledgment of this something – in this case the modern concept of what constitutes a person. This practical transcendence of modern psychology through the integration of pre-modern techniques and practices is theoretically embedded in a wider philosophical re-orientation and integration of pre-modern concepts into modern and post-modern terms. This is almost necessarily so, since the interest in altered states of consciousness or the relevance of shamanic and mystical disciplines involve significant epistemological and ontological judgments (Cf. McDermott 1993, 207). Basic work in the transpersonal regard is constituted by William James lecture-series (1901-1902) published as "The Varieties of Religious Experience". A more recent and general groundwork is Aldous Huxley's (1945) "The Perennial Philosophy," which argues the common ground or core of all religions – and through outlining this common ground by implication soars up to constitute a potential global religion on its own. However, within the contemporary transpersonal discourse, it is especially Ken Wilber who provides the wider theoretical frame with his integral theory. Besides Huxley, Wilber is in particular building on the work of Jean Gebser and Aurobindo Ghose, who independently of each other (constituting a synchronicity of its own) developed integral worldviews, where they tried to combine and integrate pre-modern, modern and post-modern worldviews, eastern and western spiritual concepts, and scientific reasoning into comprehensive theories of mind; Aurobindo Ghose with his integral yoga and Gebser with his outlines for an a-perspectivical worldview. What Gebser thus terms a-rational (Gebser 1973) is in many ways congruent with the term trans-rational. Wilber again is fundamental for Wolfgang Dietrich's work, which in many ways does for the different understandings of peace what Gebser has done for different forms of consciousness.

In the context of integrating philosophies and worldviews across time and space, Fritjof Capra has also to be mentioned. In his work "The Tao of Physics" (Capra 1975) he systematically outlines what the founding fathers of quantum mechanics already knew and had hinted at – namely how much the epistemological and ontological consequences of their findings conformed to Buddhist and Chinese cosmology – while the latter according to Jung builds on what he termed the synchronicity-principle.

At this end, I can state that what Wolfgang Dietrich has done for peace-studies is taking the consequences, and by reviewing those developments in a peace-perspective outlined the transrational peace-philosophy and practice in conformity with transpersonal psychology and integral theory – disciplines whose own implicit goals more often than not always already had been towards peace in the first place. Thus, transrational peace-studies alters or 'twist'[13] modern understandings by integrating un-modern and pre-modern practices and cosmologies – with the result being *transrational*. As such I understand myself to work in this line of tradition, when I following attempt to describe and integrate pre- and un-modern practices and assumptions in contemporary, academic terms.

[13] 'Twist' is Dr. Norbert Koppensteiner's translation of the Heideggerian term '*verwinden*' (Cf. Dietrich 2012).

2. A Story of Consciousness

Wer nicht von dreitausend Jahren
Sich weiss Rechenschaft zu geben,
Bleib im Dunkeln unerfahren,
Mag von Tag zu Tag leben.
Goethe[14]

2.1. The Model

The basic idea or postulation of the above displayed, and by Dietrich developed Diagram of Transrational Peace, is that a *persona*[15] can be described as consisting of several intra-personal dimensions or layers, where closest to the material surface of the *persona* lies the sexual layer, followed by the socio-emotional layer, the mental layer, the spiritual layer, the awareness layer and finally the epicenter (see above and cf. Dietrich 2011, 355-356). Following the tantric principle of correspondence "as within so without" each of these intra-personal layers is further described as corresponding to an inter-personal dimension in a coherent way, where every layer deeper within corresponds to a continuous wider without (or exterior). The material surface of the *persona* thus corresponds to the immediate episode on the contact border (the direct interaction), while the sexual layer corresponds to the family as the next wider inter-personal dimension, the socio-emotional to community, mental to society, spiritual to policitary, awareness to global, and finally the intra-personal epicenter to a complementary inter-personal epicenter.

By relating intra-personal structures to inter-personal structures, the diagram has already imported a part of the phylogenetic and ontogenetic parallelism, of which I simply will add another dimension. That is, inter-personal structures as families, communities and societies are not only contemporary 'building blocks' in a more or less existing and emerging post-modern, globalized world, but constitute structures which historically and contemporary have been and still are inter-personal wholes in themselves[16]. Hence and more particularly, my

[14] Cited after Neumann 1949, 1. A literal translation would be, "who cannot account for three thousand years, will remain inexperienced n the dark, only survive from day to day (my trans-lation).

[15] A *persona* (plural *personae* or *personas*), in the word's everyday usage, is a social role or a character played by an actor. The word is derived from Latin, where it originally referred to a theatrical mask. The Latin word probably derived from the Etruscan word "phersu", with the same meaning, and that from the Greek πρόσωπον (*prosōpon*). In the here presented context *persona* denotes the totality of the Apollonian material and visible form, the "mask" through which the Dionysian energy shines through and highlights thus the realization that there is something behind the "mask" (Cf. Dietrich 2008, 350).

[16] Wilber would here surely speak of 'holons', which expresses the idea that everything is a whole

argument is that every one of those inter-personal structures also corresponds to a specific way of social organization. The family as inter-personal structure corresponds thus to the social organization which I term clan society, and denotes people united and organized by kin-ship and common ancestry, generally without also forming part of larger social units such as tribes or chiefdoms. Community then corresponds to those next larger social organizations, which are built up by family-clans and typically are called tribes or chiefdoms. Here the family-clan still plays an all-important social role, but is organized with other clans into larger tribes or bands typically based on common mythology. Tribes and chiefdoms can become quite large organizations, even empires; however, defining are the logics of inclusion and exclusion procedures, which will be discussed in greater detail later on. Meanwhile and consequently, society corresponds to the organization of tribes and chiefdoms into again wider social units, of which the modern nation-state is the contemporary prime example. The artificial term *policity* corresponds in this logic then to the organization of nation-states into an again wider frame of social organization, for which the United Nations provide an example of an intent in that direction. Given that hypothetically a functioning and integrated governing UN systems would be a global encompassing phenomena, the question in how far the global layer of the Diagram would correspond to an inter-planetary organization guided by exo-politics, remains open at this point[17]. The result of this argument is that in addition to the earlier correspondence between for instance sexuality and family, I now also have another inter-personal dimension, which in this case is the clan. For all layers this means – sexual-family-clan, socio-emotional-community-tribe, mental-society-state, spiritual-policity-global government, and awareness- global – inter-planetary organization.

With the correspondence between inter-personal structures and ways of social organization, the first half of the additional dimension I want to import to the diagram of transrational peace is mentioned. The second half consist in the by Habermas (1979) and Wilber (2000) argued correspondence between (historical) ways of social organization and ways of reasoning – or what I term modes of consciousness. According to classical development psychology develops the mental capacity of a child over certain stages, which following Jean Piaget´s well-known four-stage model are called the sensorimotor (0 – 2 years old), the preoperational (2 – 7 years), the concrete operational (7 – 11 years) and the formal operational (11 years onward) (Wilber 2000, 294). Sensorimotor terms

in itself and simultaneously part of something greater. For instance, my liver is made up of molecules, where every molecule is a whole in itself but also part of something greater, which is my liver. The liver again is whole in itself but also part of a system, which is my body, etc.

[17] That this seemingly absurd proposition probably not is too far-fetched becomes evident when considering that the intra-personally corresponding layer of awareness actually is described as communication with planetary systems (Dietrich 2008, 366).

the early stage where the child practically develops its physical senses, while concrete operational is marked by magic cognition, formal operational by mythic cognition and formal operational by the capacity for abstract and rational reasoning. In Wilber's and Habermas' evolutionary narrative humans have developed the actualization of their cognitive potential in correspondence with the development of their social organization. This means that these ontogenetic stages of a child's cognitive development are set in correlation with the way of social organization within a phylogenetic narrative. People living in kin-ship based clans are thus correlated with preoperational reasoning, tribes and chiefdoms with concrete operational, and states and federations stand in a relationship with formal operational reasoning. In the following, Jean Gebser's terminology for phylogenetic consciousness development, Wilber terms the child's ontogenetic stages archaic, magic, mythic and mental in the postulated phylogenetic parallel, which I in the following will do as well. When I import this further correlation to the earlier outline, I now have four sets of corresponding pairs, each containing two intra-personal two inter-personal dimensions. The intra-personal layer of sexuality corresponds then to intra-personal magic cognition, which again corresponds to family and clan as inter-personal layers; socio-emotional corresponds to mythic cognition and tribe and community, while the intra-personal mental layer corresponds to an equally termed mental form of cognition, and inter-personally to society and a state-form of social organization[18]. Important and of interest for my work are especially these modes of cognition or consciousness, which now are brought in relation to the diagram of transrational peace. Before I can continue to outline these modes and their correspondence with the other layers and dimensions, I have to make two important distinctions and demarcations in relation to Habermas' and Wilber's evolutionary parallelism between ontogenetic and phylogenetic consciousness development.

The first distinction concerns a linear reading of development, where evolution is understood to develop towards increasing complexity and consequently to 'higher order' states. In this line of reasoning the nation-state is for instance perceived as a more complex (and thus 'better') arrangement than a tribal society – necessitating more complex cognitive processes to navigate within (formal operational reasoning in contrast to concrete operational). I do not share this reading, but are much more under the impression that tribal societies and kin-ship based organizations tend to be far more complex and demanding in terms of the social skills, interaction as well as cognitive performance they necessitate.

[18] There are more intra-personal layers and modes of consciousness which I in reference to Gebser and Wilber term *integral* and *causal,* and which correspond intra-personally to the spiritual and the awareness and inter-personal to policity and the global layer, which I for the convenience of the reader however only will introduce later.

Not only tend the range of significant persons to whom close bonds are entertained to be much greater than in modern nation-states, but the social-cognitive performance in mastering and overviewing all the relations and interrelations the kin-group is entertaining is seemingly equally astonishing. Accordingly, many generations of anthropologist have been stunned by the intricate line-age systems many so-called 'primitive' societies entertain. Many famous examples are collected among the Australian aborigines. These people who traditionally are hunters and gatherers have the most rudimentary technology, often solely based on wood. Simultaneously, they entertain line-age systems, which are so complex that it takes years for an outsider to understand (Eriksen 2007, 113). One anecdote states that when two Aborigines meet randomly in the outback, it is no question whether they are related, but how they are related and by figuring this out, they will know whether to continue together, fight each other, or just part ways (Ibid.). Family shows to be a very relative dimension, which easily can fill the size of a humans cognitive potential for social complexity. Likewise is the world a hunter and gatherer moves within not at all less complex, but on the contrary the achievement to get food on the table by walking to the super-market fades into nothing compared to the not only cognitive task which it is to hunt it down oneself. What a nation-state as social structure gains in numbers of its members, and the thereby implied benefits in case they manage to cooperate, takes its toll in other ways. This means I do not understand one form of social organization to be better or more developed than another in itself, but rather remain a marked relativist in my evaluation of these categories and strategies. Furthermore, I do not understand these categories to develop in a linear way. This will become evident when I later argue how the spiritual layer also relates to the socio-emotional and ends come to meet. This, then, will also imply that a potential global government as the UN in many ways would be a mythic construct.

Yet more important is the second distinction concerning the modes of consciousness and their alleged phylogenetic and ontogenetic parallelism. I agree with Habermas and Wilber that different forms of social organization correspond to, and are interrelated with different structures of consciousness, and the thereby implied different Cosmo-visions and predominant cognitive processes. I further agree that these collective human modes of consciousness have their parallel in the ontogeny. However, due to Habermas' and Wilber´s reduction of the collective structures onto their ontogenetic correspondence, and the thereby implied projection of a child´s cognitive development onto collective modes of consciousness, again within an evolutionary reading, I do have to make objections and important differentiations. First of all, I do not understand these developments as teleological guided processes. A child does not 'develop' all modes of consciousness, but rather touches upon all modes of consciousness in its development, so to speak in a fast track procedure. Which mode(s) of consciousness it eventually really develops and brings to flourish later on depends then on its individual biography – and not a collective phylogenetic process. Hence it is possible to find grown up individuals who predominantly live in a mythological form of consciousness guided by their socio-emotional layer, and inter-personally predominantly are occupied with people they share a form of community with, which could be a church or a sports club, even though they live in a nation-state society and potentially are able to engage and be guided by more abstract principles. This means that I agree to the existence of correspondence between cognitive states in the individual development and collective forms of consciousness in their correspondence with social organization, but object to reduce or elevate either one onto the other. Just because the German base right or Einstein's relativity-theory or Judith Butler's gender-theory build on abstract reasoning does that not imply that every twelve year old capable of abstract thought also is able to produce these constructs or even understand them. In other words, the child's or adolescents capacity for formal operational reasoning might give access to the world of abstract thought, but it does not deliver the whole abstract world or just assure a correct use of this ability. Hence, just as it would be absurd to reduce relativity-theory or Butler's work to be equal to the cognitive achievement of a twelve year old, it is equally absurd to reduce Paleolithic cultures or tribal communities who operate with magic in their reference frame to the cognitive abilities of a five-year old child. Developed magic and mythic cosmologies relate to the magic cognitions of a child just about as much as astrophysics relate to the average mathematical abilities of ten to twelve years old.

Nevertheless, studying a child's cognitive development can inform and enhance the knowledge about basic pattern in the greater collective modes of consciousness without reducing one to the other, or importing an evolutionist reading, besides demonstrating and widening the astonishing insights into correspondences already inherent in the diagram of transrational peace. My aim is to align structures of consciousness to the diagram of transrational peace, by which this theoretical tool expands and gets even more applicable. As will become evident, I am simply unpacking the existing correspondences further – and not forwarding an evolutionist agenda. Much to the contrary, my research will delve into synchronicity evidence that magic and mythic cosmovisions constitute valid interpretation systems in their own right. Finally, it has to be noted that 'the map is not the territory.' This means I do not understand the diagram and the categories I apply as objective or fixed entities describing an equally objective world. I understand them as quite subjective and culturally biased 'thought supports,' which might serve as markers for navigating in a spectrum, which defies clear boundaries.

2.2. Structures of Consciousness

In his work “Ursprung und Gegenwart” (1973) Jean Gebser differentiates between five different structures of consciousness, which he assumes that humanity has gone through and still is going through in its phylogenesis. At the 'bottom,' or as the first structure of consciousness development, Gebser identifies what he terms the archaic consciousness, followed by the magic, mythic and the mental consciousness, which, according to Gebser, is in its deficient rational phase and constitutes the current mental state. The fifth structure, which he terms integral, is according to Gebser currently emerging (Gebser 1973, 60). Once again, while I appreciate Gebser´s identification and description of different consciousness structures, which I understand as essential outlines of fundamental, historically evidenced human experiences and frames of reference, I do not share the chronological narrative onto which Gebser projects those structures. I do understand these structures as simultaneously existing areas in the latent and potential spectrum of consciousness, which historically all have been activated and fully developed in different circumstances. What I will do is to simply connect Gebser´s consciousness structures to the diagram of transrational peace, because I believe that they fit. In the following outline of the thus expanded diagram of transrational peace, I will begin every section with Gebser´s consciousness structures, before aligning them with their ontogenetic parallel and Dietrich´s layers of the diagram. In regard to terminology I will refer to the by Dietrich identified layers in their relation to the yogic chakra-model, as outlined in the first volume of Dietrich´s “Variationen über die vielen Frieden” (2008).

2.2.1. Archaic

Following Gebser the archaic structure is characterized by its pre-spatiality and pre-temporality – it is a zero-dimensional consciousness structure. As such, this zero-dimensional structure is unconscious and ego-less. There is no subject-object polarity (let alone duality), no differentiation between self and other, soul and nature, between the individual and the universe. It is a time where the soul is still dormant, and the human in complete identity with the all (Gebser 1973, 83). As a key clue towards this time, Gebser identifies a phrase of Dschuan Dsi, that in Richard Wilhelms translation says: “*Die wahrhaften Menschen der früheren Zeit schliefen traumlos*[19]” (Gebser 1973, 84). For Gebser, this is not a primitive state in the degenerative sense. Indeed, this unconscious complete identity with

[19] “The true humans of former time slept dreamless”, my translation. The idea Gebser here expresses, is that the archaic consciousness structure is equivalent with deep, dreamless sleep.

the all seems to be a mirror image of the goal of yogic and spiritual development termed non-duality – a point I will come back to.

2.2.1.1. Sensorimotor

In its ontogenetic correlation, this stage of consciousness relates to the period of sensorimotor intelligence, which is where the newborn learns first habits, conditioning and circular reactions, such as sucking its thumb (Piaget 1972, 54). In terms of consciousness, this stage is by development psychologists described as primary indissociation, 'oceanic adualism' (Arieti), or 'primary narcissism' (Wilber 2000, 295). The infant´s self is not differentiated in relation to its surroundings (complete identity with the surroundings), and only by for instance biting itself and feeling pain, and biting a blanket without feeling pain, it slowly learns to differentiate the physical self from the physical other. It is in Piaget´s terms a stage of pure autism, where no objective observation or reasoning is possible: there is only a perpetual play which transforms perceptions and creates situations in accordance with the subject´s pleasure (for Wilber the reason the Romantics search back to this original state – and indeed a description of heaven) (Ibid., 301).

> From an ontological viewpoint, what corresponds to this manner of thinking is primitive psychological causality, probably a form that implies magic proper: the belief that any desire whatsoever can influence objects, the belief in the obedience of external things. Magic and autism are therefore two different sides of one and the same phenomenon – the confusion between the self and the world... (Piaget 1977, 151-152).

2.2.1.2. Muladhara

In the chakra-psychology this stage correlates to *muladhara*, the first chakra, which intra-personally relates to the physical body and its material functions such as nutrition, metabolism and excretion, birth and reproduction, breath and death (Dietrich 2008, 362). Fittingly, Dietrich describes the egoic aspect of this stage as overindulgence (Dietrich uses the more fitting German word "Maßlosigkeit") (Ibid.). This 'lack of measurement' corresponds to Gebser´s term of zero-dimensional, as there is no sense of dimensions at this stage. A later imbalance on this stage expresses itself thus as greed, which is a hindrance for the experience of peace. Dietrich remarks in this regard that for a conscious person the opposite of have is not not-have, but not-wanting-to-have (Dietrich 2008, 363). Hence, from a peace-psychological viewpoint, a materially rich person can suffer as much as a materially poor person, when the attitude is set on have - something no material wealth ever can satisfy. Consequently, the yogic chakra-psychology recommend moderation in regard to material consumption, not because it is morally wrong, but since overindulgence is a psychological hindrance towards the development of a sense of self and the experience of peace (Cf. Ibid.).

On an interpersonal level, this stage conforms to what Gestalt therapy calls the episode on the contact-border. By Contact-border is meant this physical border that the infant slowly experiences and learns to differentiate, and that readily can be experienced by the senses. It is the world of the five senses, and the only valid reality for positivists, who consequently get in trouble as soon as it gets a little bit deeper and wider, as on the next level. Since the contact-border marks the physical surface of the episode, the contact between different parties and agents in peace-work is here marked by superficial *role* and *cliché,* which expresses itself in professional distance (Cf. Dietrich 2011, 363). Peace-work solely operating on this level is consequently concerned with the physical survival as in disaster operations, and similar first aid emergencies. As soon as the contact goes beyond the mere episode, static adherence to the professional distance and role would gradually question personal authenticity, and thus become a blockage on the contact-border, where for a realization of a peace-process in a transrational sense, the life-energy of the whole being has to flow (Ibid.).

2.2.2. Magic

According to Gebser, the magic consciousness steps out of the zero-dimensional structure of the archaic *identity* into one-dimensional *unity*. The one-dimensional unity is still characterized by unconscious space- and timelessness, I-world-god are experienced as energetic points, which are in an interrelationship, and interchangeable (Gebser 1973, 87). The symbol of this structure is the point, it is a point-consciousness with the *pars pro toto* as its motto, in which one entity can represent other entities. An example could be the cow as representation of the great mother, which simultaneous is the world. These points can be interchanged at will. It is a world of pure, but meaningful chance – in other words the world of synchronicity; a world in which all things and persons are interrelated, but the not-yet centered ego is dispersed over the world of phenomena (Ibid., 88). In a sense one may say that in this structure consciousness was not yet in the human, but still resting in the world. Habermas explains:

> Apparently the magical-animistic representational world of paleolithic societies was very particularistic and not very coherent. The ordering representations of mythology (i.e., early mythology and not the complex mythology that is the next stage <A/N>.) first made possible the construction of a complex of analogies in which natural and social phenomena were intervowen and could be transformed into one another. In the egocentric world conception of the child at the

> preoperational level of thought, these phenomena are made relative to the center of the child's ego; similarly, in sociomorphic worldviews they are made relative to the center of the tribal group (Habermas 1979, 104).

An example of how the interchangeability of points practically functions, the transformation and interrelation between social and natural phenomena, and how the ego is dispersed over the world of phenomena is provided in the following case. In his book "Unknown Africa," Leo Frobenius describes a hunting rite, which he observed in the Congo jungle:

> [M]embers of the hunting tribe of Pygmies (three men and a woman) drew a picture of an antelope in the sand before they started out at dawn to hunt antelopes. With the first ray of sunlight that fell on the sand, they intended to "kill" the antelope. Their first arrow hit the drawing unerringly in the neck. Then they went out to hunt and returned with a slain antelope. Their death-dealing arrow hit the animal in exactly the same spot, where hours before, the other arrow had hit the drawing... [H]aving fulfilled its magic purpose... this arrow was then removed from the drawing with an accompanying ritual designed to ward off any evil consequences of the murder from the hunters. After that was done, the drawing itself was erased. (Cited after Gebser 1973, 89).

Gebser identifies several characteristics of the magic structure illustrated by this scene. The egolessness is expressed first of all in the fact that the responsibility for the murder, committed by the group-ego against a part of nature, is attributed to a power already felt to be 'standing outside,' which is the sun. It is not the pygmies' arrow that kills, but the first arrow of the sun that falls on the animal, and of which the real arrow is only a symbol (nowadays, of course, one would interpret it just the other way around and say: the sun's ray is a symbol of the arrow). In this linking of the responsibility of the hunters' group-ego (assuming the form of four human beings performing the rite) with the sun — which, because of its brightness, must be considered a symbol of consciousness — it is clear to what extent the capacity for consciousness of these human beings is still on the outside or connected with the out-side (Gebser 1973, 91). With the Pygmies in their egolessness, the moral consciousness that they must bear responsibly, deriving from a clearly conscious ego (in the sense of I or self-awareness), is still attributed to the sun. Their ego (and with it an essential part of their soul) is still scattered over the world, like the light of the sun. This leads directly to the second characteristic: point-like unity. This is expressed in the visible interchangeability of the real and the symbolic causative element; that is, in equating the ray of sunlight and the arrow. According to Gebser, at the basis of this point-like unity lies a natural vital nexus, and not a rational causal one (Gebser 1973, 92). This point-related unity in which each and every thing intertwines and is interchangeable, becomes apparent when the symbolic murder in a rite, performed before a hunt, coincides exactly with the actual one committed by the hunter. In the spaceless and timeless world of the magic structure, this constitutes a working unity, which operates without a causal nexus, and for Gebser constitutes an effective reality (Gebser 1973, 48).

Spacelessness and timelessness are thus further characteristics of the magic structure, and it is according to Gebser only in a world of space- and timelessness that the point-like unity has effective reality character (Ibid.). They are the reason why every point (a thing, event, or action) can be symbolically and effectively interchanged with another point, independently of time and place, and of any rational causal connection. Apparently, every point can not only be linked with any other point, but is rather identified with it - one can substitute for the other completely (the pars pro toto) (Cf. Ibid., 92). It is the lack of spatial and temporal separation that allows things, events, or actions to be effectively correlated or to influence each other in a non-causal or pre-causal manner. Gebser notes that this unifying connection must seem unreal from a modern, rational perspective, since this connecting proceeds in the vegetative psychic energetic, while it loses its effect as soon as rational 'causalisation' sets in, since the activation of consciousness disrupts the unconsciously connecting psychic energetic and dismantles its effectivity (Ibid.). I have to partly disagree with Gebser on this latter point; since synchronistic phenomena show that rational 'causalisation' does not lose the effect of this truly 'magic' connecting. What rational 'causalisation' does, is to interpret and emphasize the same happenings on the contact-border of the episode differently – and consequently reacts differently and breaks with the inherent logic of the magic causality. Following is an example to illustrate what I mean. Lucien Levy-Bruhl relates a paradigmatic historical incident from former German West Africa, where a chief named Kanime from the Ovambi tribe was having an ox prepared for work. Just as they were about to to pierce its nostrils, the animal tossed its horns and put out someones eye.

> They said at once that the man who had lost his eye had been bewitched. They consulted the wizard, and as he had to discover who had woven the spell, he indicated one of Kanime´s servants as the guilty party. When condemned to death, this man ran away, but Kanime pursued him on horseback, overtook him and killed him (Levy-Bruhl 1923, 47-48).

Rational 'causalisation', which is marked by its enlightened ruling out of 'supernatural forces,' would see several causal chains over time that have come to meet, the most important ones being the party of men who, as men used to do, prepare oxen and pierce their nostrils, and the other one being the life of the ox which, as oxen do, more often than not when they get domesticated they have their nostrils pierced and - also - toss their horns. The putting out of the eye would in this perspective be interpreted as unfortunate, but in itself a rather meaningless accident, and if at all going deeper in its analysis, attribute the incident to the ill-will of the ox, and rather carelessness on part of the man. The interpretation would keep within those chronological causal lines, while the logical consequences in a rational perspective would be to either kill this particular ox, or to alter the practice of piercing in the future - and most likely both. In the magical perspective, there is evidently a different reason for the particular meeting of those causal lines that culminate in the putting out of the eye. Here, the visible episode on the contact-border is *a priori* ordered by an *invisible* intention or background. The reaction following the incident reveals that the tribesmen are solely interested in this presumed invisible background, the meaning-connections in the moment, with no regard for the causal chains over time – a regard, which if Gebser is right about the space- and timelessness of this structure, also would be impossible. The relation between the invisible background/intention and the visible episode on the contact-border is thus one of quality or form – or in another word; meaning. The true incident here is the ill will of Kanime´s servant, which finds its symbolical reflection in the putting out of the eye by the ox in the visible episode. The violent and paradigmatic killing of the presumed perpetrator might further illustrate how vulnerable magic consciousness is to invisible intentions and ill-will. The danger of getting bewitched is ever present and feared in this consciousness, and since there is no safeguard against bewitchment from within this consciousness; perpetrators, whether real or not, usually were killed to prevent further accidents from this source (Cf. Levy-Bruhl 1923, 50). It should be noted that witchcraft not necessarily denotes a conscious casting of spells or other ritual action – but mostly unconscious 'evil' intentions, which potentially every human can produce. What Gebser describes as the disruptive effect of consciousness on magic has thus rather to be understood as an ignoring of the unifying connections of the vegetative psychic energetic. Since consciousness has to do with differentiating in time and space, while these unifying connections proceed in a pre-spatial and pre-temporal manner, it is quite understandable that rational 'causalisation' is ignorant of these connections. I again agree with Gebser when he attributes the phenomena studied by parapsychology to this spaceless and timeless structure, which, like all previous structures, remains active in the psyche, and is capable of being accessed. This merging with nature, which in its spacelessness and timelessness also connotes a remarkable boundlessness, explains for Gebser the well-founded powers of the magic man — powers which survive today in the form of human mediums. It is explained in part by an elimination of consciousness, which obscures or blacks out the ego, and causes it to revert to a spaceless-timeless 'unconscious participation- in the group soul. All magic, even today, occurs according to Gebser in this natural-vital, egoless, spaceless and timeless sphere (Ibid. 101).

2.2.2.1. Preoperational

I would at this point like to emphasize that Gebser, contrary to Wilber and (development) psychology generally, accredits the magic consciousness validity and reality within its own range – which is an assessment I share, and a circumstance that also Jung´s findings in relation to synchronicity underscore, and shall therefore be discussed in greater detail later on. Wilber, who writes and reasons from a strict mental/rational three-dimensional perspective, exemplary for a modern rational mode of reasoning where the Aristotelian "*tertium non datur*" is the rule, therefore correctly criticizes from his perspective this magical thinking for confusing different *holons*, either because they share similar agency (the law of similarity) or because they share similar communions (the law of contact) (Wilber 2000, 304). In Wilber´s own words:

> [M]agical cognition is not yet capable of grasping the notion of a *holon.* It does not set whole and part in a rich network of *mutual* relationships, but short-circuits the process by merely collapsing or confusing various wholes and parts – what Piaget calls syncretism and juxtaposition (again, similarity and contiguity). Magical cognition, then, is of fused and confused wholes and parts, and not mutually related wholes and parts. These "fused networks" of "syncretic wholes" *appear* very holistic (or "holographic"), but are actually not very coherent, and do not even match the already available sensorimotor evidence (Ibid.).

What Wilber does here is basically being 'mental-centristic,' when he evaluates the ontogenetic development, which at this stage is termed preoperational. In this stage or phase the child slowly learns to differentiate its emotional self from emotional objects. In the beginning, there is no differentiation between the child's own emotions and especially the motherly one(s) (point-like unity). Wilber refers to this phase as the "separation-individuation phase," or the integration of a stable emotional self (whereas the former phase was the stabilization and integration of the physical self), because the infant emerges from its emotional fusion with the (m)other (Wilber, 302). By around age three, if all has gone well, the young child has a stable and coherent physical and emotional self and language has begun to emerge – but magical cognitions continue to dominate the entire early preoperational period (2 – 4 years). During this period, the newly emerging images and symbols do not merely represent objects; they are thought to be concretely part of the things they represent.

> Up to the age 4-5, [the child] thinks that he is "forcing" or compelling the moon to move; the relation takes on an aspect of dynamic participation or of magic. From 4 to 5 he is more inclined to think that the moon is trying to follow him: the relation is animistic. Closely akin to this participation is *magical causality,* magic being in many respects simple participation: the subject regards his gestures, his thoughts, or the objects he handles, as charged with efficacy, thanks to the very participations which he establishes between those gestures, etc, and the things around him. Thus a certain word acts upon a certain thing; a certain gesture will protect one from a certain danger; a certain white pebble will bring about the growth of water lilies, and so on... (Piaget, quoted after Wilber 2000, 303-304).

Wilber compares this magical thinking to Freud´s notions of *displacement* and *condensation*, explaining that in displacement, two different objects are equated or linked because they share similar parts or predicates (a relation of similarity), while condensation relates different aspects because they exist in the same space (a relation of contiguity: a lock of hair of a great warrior contains in condensed form the power of the warrior) (Ibid., 304). Notwithstanding what Freud actually meant by those terms, Wilber does here indeed describe the fundamentals of so-called *sympathetic magic* as outlined by Sir James George Frazer in "The Golden Bough" (1994):

> If we analyze the principles of thought on which magic is based, they will probably be found to resolve themselves into two: first, that like produces like, or that an effect resembles its cause; and, second, that things which have once been in contact with each other continue to act on each other at a distance after the physical contact has been severed. The former principle may be called the Law of Similarity, the latter the Law of Contact or Contagion. From the first of these principles, namely the Law of Similarity, the magician infers that he can produce any effect he desires merely by imitating it: from the second he infers that whatever he does to a material object will affect equally the person with whom the object was once in contact, whether it formed part of his body or not (Frazer 1994 [1889], 35).

This by Frazer described form of magical reason is strikingly similar to Gebser´s magical consciousness, where the interchangeability of points relates to the law of similarity and the *pars pro toto* to the law of contact. As Gebser pointed out, these connections seem to work prior to space and time, and seem thus not causally connected but by what Gebser termed the 'vital connex' in the vegetative psychic energetic. That this 'vital connex' also appears as an emotional factor is indicated by the circumstance that the child here is differentiating its emotional self from the physical self, for which reason this 'vital connex' also could be termed emotional connections. That these emotional connections often constitute literal or real emotional fusions and participations – and not simply cognitive confusions as Wilber suggests – is underscored by Jung´s theory of synchronicity, which I will treat later on.

Again, because I assume that space and time transcending emotional connections exist and pattern events into meaningful episodes, and that the by many pre-modern people claimed connections, such as those between hunting rituals and the actual hunt, often constitute valid interpretations within their own logic, I do not assume that every claim in this direction is correct, just as every mathe-matical calculation does not reach correct results, albeit basic mathematical skills are mastered. What I assume is that, very roughly put, magic consciousness can be described as a pre-egoic, pre-spatial and pre-temporal state of emotional fusion (not confusion) with the surroundings, for which reason it does not interpret events in a three-dimensional space and time frame of reference, but in a one-dimensional unitary fashion, where phenomena are set in inter-relationship according to their emotional quality and analogy in the moment. I further assume that this constitutes an experienceable reality plane, which not only is character-istic for Paleolithic and Neolithic as well as more recent people typically living in kinship-based family clans with shamanism as religious institution, but also exists as latent or active layer in every human and has its ontogenetic parallel in the preoperational phase. Furthermore, do I find reason to suggest that pre-egoic, emotional fusion, in many ways also is characteristic for any functioning family.

2.2.2.2. Svadisthana

After the discussion above, it is no wonder that the second chakra, *svadisthana,* inter-personally is associated with the family and intra-personally with sexuality, feelings and emotions (Dietrich 2011, 364-368). Dietrich describes it as the place where memories are converted into emotions. In this perspective, emotions are energetically charged memory-structures in the present. Fear and physical pain are incentives for egoical actions, while bravery is not the opposite of fear, but just a different appearance of the same *energy* – as virtually all emotions are. To this belongs especially also the wish to reproduce (past) experiences of lust and pleasure. Sexual energy reproduces itself, as long as it remains unbalanced and unconscious, and with this desire that can lead to aggression and adherence to violence (Dietrich 2008, 363). However, emotions and (sexual) energy can do more than blur the perception of the here and now, and reproduce it self and biologically reproduce physical bodies. As Dietrich points out, this is the level in which elicitive peace-work corresponds to (shamanic) *healing* (Cf. Dietrich 2011, 364). Traditional healing on this level has everything to do with 'vitality' and energy, but not so much with the sexual aspect of this energy, as with the effects that emotions and vitality magically manifest in their surroundings through the 'vital connex' in the vegetative psychic energetic - e.g. *synchronicity*. It should further be noticed that Gebser´s 'magical human' and the associated societies are the same which Dietrich terms *energetic* societies, presumably often matriarchally organized and characterized by (energetic) peace out of fertility/harmony (Cf. Dietrich 2008). The term *energetic* fits very well in this developed perspective, since *energy* in this context means exactly what Gebser terms the 'vegetative psychic energetic' responsible for the vital connex. This vitality is exactly the *energy* which Dietrich invokes again and again as the Dionysian counterpart to Apollonian form, and which humans experience as feelings and emotions – and especially also sexuality, with its search for lustful unification. How this relates to the family probably needs no mention. In this perspective, the sexual act reveals itself as the magic act per se.

Since also matter and form are forms of energy, I could state that the 'primal' energy, which at the archaic level or first chakra is differentiated form-wise (the physical body, form and not-form), at this second level is further differentiated into the polarity of form and feeling. Feelings and emotions then, and the better word is probably vitality or *energy*, appears to be the decisive factor in magic (and the better word here is probably 'synchronistic') connections as already indicated. This circumstance is not a new idea, and for instance Avicenna (980 – 1037) and Albertus Magnus (1200 – 1280) have already written on the connection between magic and emotion.

> I found (in relation to magic) a plausible explanation in the sixth book of Avicenna´s Naturalia, that the soul holds a certain power (virtus) to change things, and that the other things are subdued to the soul; this is, when the soul is raptured in a great excess of love or hate or similar (quando ipsa fertur in magnum amoris excessum aut odii aut alicuius talium). So, when the soul of a human gets in to a great excess of any form of passion, one can experimentally determine, that it (the excess) (magically) binds things together and changes them into that very direction towards which it strives (fertur in grandem excessum alicuius passionis invenitur experimento manifesto quod ipse ligat res et alterat ad idem quod desiderat et diu non credidi illud), and I have for a long time not believed it, but after studying nigromantic books and such about magic symbols (imaginum) and magic, I found that (really) the emotionality (affecto) of the human soul is the main root of all these things, be it either, that it through great emotions alters its body and other things for which it strives, or that through its inherent dignity the other things are subdued (to the soul), or be it that with such a great excess the fitting sideral hour coincides or the astrological situation or another power runs parallel, and we (thus) believe that it really is the power of the soul which causes these things... who thus wants to know the secret about this, and how to cause that, has to know that everyone can magically influence everything, when he gets into a great excess... (Albertus Magnus, ca 1488, cited and translated after Jung 1952, 36-37).

Albertus Magnus here speculates whether it actually is the human soul, which is another term for the emotional self, that causes these 'magic' patterning of events into the direction it strives for, or whether the soul rather coincides with the macrocosmic situation, as for instance the astrological hour, and thus in reality only is a pawn in the hands of greater constellations, while it then only from the ego-perspective seems to be oneself that is the root of these patterns[20]. This question would also occupy C. G. Jung about five hundred years later. Interesting and relevant at this point is to note that the fact that Albertus Magnus speculations on these questions indicates that he himself not dwells in a magic consciousness, but in virtue of these abstract reflections is emancipated from its spell and settled in a mental ego-consciousness. Magic consciousness is in its pre-egoic state unconscious of itself being enchanted by the emotional forces. As just pointed out above, this is a problematic condition from a peace philosophical perspective, since the unconsciously re-produced desire leads to aggression and violence. The necessary abstraction and transcendence of the magic structure occurs in the next layer, which I following Gebser term mythic.

[20] While this reminds of the joke about training cats, who actually follow commands, as long as the commands follow what the cat already is doing by itself – what Albertus Magnus here really speculates about is the question of free will.

2.2.2.3. The Shift from Preoperational to Concrete Operational

As the child moves from early preoperational (2-4 years: magic) to late preoperational (4-7 years: magic/mythic) similar types of magic cognition dominate awareness, while typically one major shift occurs; continued interaction with the world and rising awareness eventually lead the child to realize that his or her thoughts do not egocentrically control, create, or govern the world alone. Piaget describes this shift accordingly:

> During the first stage [early preoperational] all the explanations given are psychological, phenomenistic, finalistic and magical. During the second stage [magic-mythic] the explanations are artificialist, animistic and dynamic, and the magical forms tends to diminish (Piaget 1977, 143).

Wilber describes this shift pointedly:

> The first stage is magical: we make the clouds move by walking. The clouds obey us at a distance. The average age of this stage is 5. The second stage is both artificialist and animistic. Clouds move because God or men make them move. The average age of this stage is 6 (Wilber 2000, 306-307).

This means the omnipotent magic of the child is transferred to other subjects – maybe I cannot make the world cater for my needs, but Mummy (or God or Santa Claus) can – and mythology according to developmental psychology is born. Philip Cowan points out,

> During the [late preoperational] stage, there is still confusion between physical and personal causality; the physical world appears to operate much the way people do. All of these examples [show that late preoperational] children have already developed elaborate mythologies about cosmic questions such as the nature of life (and death) and the cause of wind... Further, these mythologies show many similarities from child to child across cultures and do not seem to have been directly taught by adults (Cowan 1978, 168).

The circumstance, that similar mythologies arise in separate cultures and people, and also later on in life and not only in children, shall be investigated further later on, when dealing with Jungian psychology. Relevant at this point is to note that magical cognition is altered and diminished in the late preoperational stage, but continues to influence and exist (in the forming of symbols and mental images), just as mythological cognition diminishes but continues to exist in other cognitive structures. The important point here, however, which Wilber tries to make and Gebser also made in his model, regards the correlating ego-awareness development. When infants and young children by development psychologists are described as narcissistic and egocentric, this does not mean that they selfishly only think about themselves, but to the contrary, that they are unable to think about themselves.

> The egocentric child is unable to differentiate himself from the rest of the world; he has not separated himself out from others or from objects. Thus he feels that others share his pain or his pleasure, that his mumblings will inevitably be understood, that his perspective is shared by all persons, that even animals and plants partake of his consciousness. In playing hide-and-seek he will "hide" in broad view of other persons, because his egocentrism prevents him from recognizing that others are aware of his location. The whole course of human development can be viewed as a continuing decline in egocentrism... (Gardner 1972, 63).

What Gebser correspondingly terms egolessness does thus not denote altruistic selflessness, but the lack of stable ego-awareness. I here agree with Wilber on the point that human consciousness and psychological development can be described as a decline in egocentrism through continued decentering, differentiation and integration. The egocentrism characteristic for the child in the sensorimotor and preoperational stage continues to decline during accomplished development. While the sensorimotor stage is characterized by a differentiation of the physical self from the physical surroundings, the preoperational stage can be described as a differentiation of the biological and emotional self from the surroundings. The next phase then, concrete operational, has to do with belonging and community – it is the differentiation of the social self from other social selves and social *role* awareness.

In regard to the collective shift from magic to mythic, it is an undecided question whether the mythic representational system followed societal organization or vice versa – or whether both just stand in a meaningful relationship. Habermas and his collaborators argue evolutionary that ecologically conditioned problems such as land scarcity and population density, or problems of social distribution of wealth, have overloaded the adaptive capacity limited by the kinship principle of organization (magic-consciousness) and forced some neolithic societies to use cognitive potentials in their worldviews and institutionalize an administration of justice on a conventional level (Habermas 1979, 162). Thus, for example, the war chief was empowered to adjudicate cases of conflict no longer only according to the distribution of power, but according to socially recognized norms grounded in tradition. Law was no longer only that on which the parties could agree (Ibid.). What is certain is that the emergence of complex mythologies also enabled humans to organize societies beyond blood lineage, and gain a wider integrative capacity. While the preconventional/magic communities centered around common ancestor (kinship), these emerging societies center around a common ruler and/or mythology. Wilber follows this understanding, when he states:

> The transition to *societies organized through a state* required the relativization of tribal identities and the construction of a more abstract [meaning less bodybound] identity that no longer based the membership of individuals on common descent but on belonging in common to a territorial organization. This took place first through identification with the figure of a ruler who could claim close connection and privileged access to the mythological originary powers. In the framework of mythological worldviews the integration of different tribal traditions was

> accomplished through a large-scale, syncretic expansion of the world of the gods – a solution that proved to be rather unstable. It wasn't that magical-animistic societies had no mythologies, for they did. It was simply that, as Joseph Campbell explained, the rise of the first early states was marked by an explosion of codified mythologies – an enormous differentiation/integration of mythic motifs – and Habermas's point is that these mythologies became a large part of the integrating structures for society (i.e., providing both cultural meaning and social integration). As we saw, in the previous or magical structure, personal identity was *natural* or body-based, and collective identity was likewise kinship or blood-bound, particularly through a common ancestor. Without a common ancestor (or kinship lineage), there was no way to socially integrate various interests. With the rise of the mythological structure, however, personal identity switched to a *role* identity in a society of a common *political* (not genetically related) ruler, and this ruler was given legitimacy not because of blood ties but because of his (or sometimes her) special relation to mythological gods/goddesses - "mythic membership. (Wilber 2000, 242-243).

If I cut away Wilber´s functionalist implications, where he seemingly believes a Mastermind wanted to implement a state and thus invented mythology in order to integrate the masses, what I see and find plausible is a correspondence between mythological representative systems and wider tribal federations, which necessitates and activates the always already latently existing mythic layer.

2.2.3. Mythic

Jean Gebser describes the transition from the magic to the mythical consciousness-structure as the development of a sense of time, which has a natural quality. Closely connected to this sense of time is the 'soul.' Time and soul are for Gebser expressions of psychic energy, which constitute the preforms of matter. Where magic consciousness becomes conscious of nature, the mythical consciousness becomes conscious of the soul. Gebser recognizes the mythical structure in the seasonal-rites of the old civilizations. In astronomy and calendars of those cultures comes the preceding magic consciousness to an end. The rhythms of nature are now experienced as temporal phenomena (Gebser 1973, 105). The magical consciousness freed itself from nature, and through this deliverance from nature distanced also the yet unconscious ego itself from nature, and consciously realized nature as an "other." The mythical structure now discovers in an opposite movement the world within the human, which is the soul. The scattered point of the *pars pro toto* gains a two-dimensional structure, which can be expressed in the self-enclosing circle or the ouroboros, the symbol of the soul. The circle encompasses all polarities and binds them balancing together: thus returns in an eternal circle the year over its polar manifestations of summer and winter back onto itself, just as the course of the sun through midnight and noon encompasses light and dark. The mythical structure recognizes the opposite poles in nature, and places heaven and sun as opposite poles to the earth, and heaven as opposite to the underworld, so that the in the magical fight realized earth is enfolded by the two polar realities of the soul: the underworldly Hades and the overworldly Olympus. Since the soul has this mirror-quality, it does not only contain natural temporality, but implies also the non-temporal, the Eternal, which is related to either heaven or hell (Gebser 1973, 107). The conduct of the god or the human in the mythical consciousness-structure is characterized by the closing of the senses, the silent look-within and the listening within. The result is the mythos, the word as the expression of the inner vision. Thus is the word always the mirror of silence, the myth the mirror of the soul. Only the blind side enables the seeing. And since everything that belongs to the soul has this mirror-character, it is not only marked by natural temporality, but also always related to the heaven; the soul is a mirror of heaven – and hell. Thus closes the mythical circle of time – soul – myth – heaven and hell myth – soul – time (Ibid. 104-105).

2.2.3.1. Concrete Operational

In the concrete operational stage (which Wilber terms "mythic/rational") a differentiation of body, emotion and mind sets in, and a beginning ego-awareness increases, which thus means a decline of egocentrism. Piaget considered the concrete stage a major turning point in the child's cognitive development, because it marks the beginning of logical or operational thought. The child is now mature enough to use logical thought or operations (i.e. rules) but can only apply logic to physical objects (hence *concrete* operational) (McLeod 2009). Children become better at conservation tasks. This means that the child understands that although the appearance of something changes, the thing itself does not. They gain the abilities of conservation (number, area, volume, orientation) and reversibility. Their thinking is more organized and rational. They can solve problems in a logical fashion, but are typically not able to think abstractly or hypothetically. In terms of identity formation a shift from egocentrism towards sociocentrism is evident, which means that the child learns to understand and differentiate its own and others social *roles* (i.e. mythic membership). This then is the proper mythic stage, which for Wilber and Habermas structurally correlates to the mental processes found among native people around the world at the early stages of colonialism by missionaries and anthropologists. That this, seen from their ethnocentric perspective, is not too far-fetched seems empirically evident. Lucien Levy-Bruhl quotes in this regard Jesuit missionaries, who were the first to see the Indians dwelling in the eastern parts of Northern America, and stated:

> We are forced to the conclusion that the Iroquois are incapable of reasoning like the Chinese and other civilized races to whom we set forth the belief in God and His truth... The Iroquois is not influenced by reason. His direct perception of things is the only light which guides him. The

> incentives to belief which theology is accustomed to use in order to convince the most hardened free-thinkers are not listened to here, where our most profound truths are declared to be lies. They usually believe only what they see. (Levy-Bruhl 1923, 21).

After attesting the same dynamics for the Greenlanders, Levy-Bruhl states that:

> It is not to be doubted that the Greenlanders, when following the avocations necessary to their existence, do reason, and that they employ means which are sometimes complicated, in order to arrive at the ends they are seeking. But these mental processes are not independent of the material objects, which induce them, and they come to an end as soon as their aim has been attained. They are never exercised on their own account, and that is why they do not seem to us to rise to the level of what we properly term "thought" (Levy-Bruhl 1923, 22-23).

This mental habit, which rules out abstract thought and reasoning, seems to be met with in a large number of what back then was termed 'uncivilized communities,' and constitutes according to Levy-Bruhl a characteristic and essential trait of 'primitive mentality' (Ibid, 29). As Levy-Bruhl later points out, and which in Gebser´s logic would constitute the inevitable mythical opposite of this adherence on concrete circumstances, is that the reason for incidents and accidents always are interpreted as due to mystical, invisible forces such as witchcraft, and even when causal connections are pointed out are they considered of minor importance, and at best as instrument for the occult powers (Ibid. 37).

2.2.3.2. A Note on Freedom

Since the mythological stage no longer is the world of magic unity, but in Gebser´s sense one of mythological polar enclosedness, it is only consequential that the concept of freedom at this stage begins to be increasingly differentiated and abstracted from its earlier unity with sexuality, love and fertility towards (and here the closeness and smooth transition of what here is described as stages once more becomes visible) a person from one's own clan or tribe, a familiar friend and beloved person - as opposed to a stranger, war prisoner or slave (Etymologisches Wörterbuch des Deutschen 1993, 102). The focus shifts (Wilber would say elevated – but that is as argued a matter of taste and I do rather regard it as a horizontal expansion) from the unity of freedom with Frej and Freja, denoting romantic love, fertility and vitality towards a societal context, a question of social role and who is inside and who is outside the mythologically argued social circle – who is friend and who is foe. Mythologically, this shift is expressed in Nordic mythology by the Æsir – Vanir War(s), where eventually the Vanir twins Frej and Freja in a trickery exchange are incorporated into the Æsir group living in Asgard. Significantly, the Vanir, a godly race who seem much closer connected to the earth, have more undifferentiated archaic/magic matriarchal levels as indicated by for instance the incestuous relationship between Frej and Freja (which as well denotes a beginning differentiation of a form of archaic androgyny), and besides their obvious connection to fertility and unity, they (the Vanir) are not defeated or extinct by the now from a human perspective dominating Asir, but incorporated and embedded into the Asir agenda. This dynamic is also based on all different levels here described, and could also not be different – as for instance, to take a parallel example, the earth could survive without humans on it, while the relatively newcomers on this planet, humans, could not survive without the supporting and much older earth. Equally, each consciousness-structure and chakra builds on, incorporates and differentiates the preceding ones, without making extinct or dissolving the functions and meanings of those earlier structures – but to the contrary, remains in a vital, meaningful and necessary interrelation. Thus Odin, the mythic father of the gods and symbol of patriarchal domination, frequently visits the Norns (old women sitting at the roots of the world tree Yggdrasil weaving humans life-threads) for counsel, and applies magic - especially to cunningly outlive his virility. In terms of freedom, the literally vital and pivotal point in its meaning of fertility and (magic) unity remains active, but another layer of meaning, another pivotal point is added and differentiated towards which here the focus of awareness now turns, and which is the mythological polar opposite of Us and Them – and in other variations of the binary mythic circle day and night, man and woman, heaven and hell, life and death. However, these categories are in the mytho-logic not dualistic opposites, but polarities and as such intimately connected – as for instance visible in the constant struggle but also intermarriage between the Jötir and Æsir in Nordic mythology, and the relation between Odin and Loki – where the latter seems to be a sort of shadow or 'evil twin' of the former, and thus together form two sides of one character (...). Interesting, albeit somewhat rhetorically, is the similarity to the popular notion of the "free world" during the Cold War era, where the "free world" were the US and its allies (friends and them at peace with) vs. the Communist Bloc. The old Game repeated, where both "sides" performed as the shadow aspect of the other within the mythologically closed circle.

With increased differentiation, abstraction, and internal distance in historical societies the sociogenesis of the term freedom changes accordingly. Thus, in ancient Greek and ancient Rome the act of *manumissio* (literally: to sent away from ones hand) describes a slave-owner freeing his slave into a freedman – or *libertus* in Roman terms (Bauman 1988, 46). But their social status was completely negative – they were not slaves anymore, neither full-born citizens, and still obliged towards their former master (Ibid.). While I do not want to neglect that the *manumittere* more often than not might have involved affection, erotic love and friendship, what we do see is the transformation of free-dom into a more juridical term, meaning the attainment of more rights and privileges contrasted to slaves. While this still has the connotation of taking an outsider (the slave) into the in-group, though not as an equal, it also seems closer to a more contemporary understanding of free as the opposite of legal restrictions.

2.2.3.3. Manipura

Since the chakra-psychology indeed seems correlative with the ontogenetic and collective consciousness structures as I claimed at the beginning, the third chakra, *manipura*, fittingly relates to community/social competence and intellect (Cf. Dietrich 2008, 363). Social competence or communality has exactly everything to do with knowing the roles, narratives, conducts, hierarchies and who is in and who is out of the different groups – and at the least to know the own place and expectations towards the personal role. In regard to intellect, it has to be noted that this term as used here relates to mental tasks performed by using time – by this I mean to stop and withdraw from the immediate and direct engagement with the episode on the contact-border in order to perform mental tasks – which at this stage are concrete operational, as outlined above meaning that they orientate along concrete objects. This is different than the 'emotional intelligence'[21] operating at the magical level, which is of immediate result and character, and in its more pure form establishes immediate, energetic connections between different points, mentally as well as operating with symbols and images. The modern claim that mythological reasoning is more intelligent than magical, albeit still less intelligent then modern rationality (as for instance Wilber does) believes (quite mythologically) that the own standpoint and measure is the (only) right and true one. It would be more correct to state that the different forms and states of intelligence can and do different things. Intelligence is here concretely measured by their degree in which they withdraw from the concrete episode and by this accumulate time – which at some point, when the withdrawal goes too far, as well becomes a deficit – as currently is the case in the contemporary state of the art (and topic in the next level). However, when intelligence is used as denoting the ability and degree of mental abstraction, then this is indeed the structure where intelligence attains momentum and has everything to do with the awareness and interplay of polar opposites and

21 My usage of the term 'emotional intelligence' has not to be confused with the meaning it has in development psychology, as especially developed by Howard Gardner, where it denotes the ability to differentiate and recognize own and others feelings and also influence others feelings. In the magic consciousness this is exactly contrary.

symbolic correspondences – Claude Levi-Strauss′ grit to analyze myth - and Gebser′s birth of the soul, which simultaneously is the birth of time.

As this chakra intrapersonally relates to (social) intelligence and interpersonally to communality, the aspects at this level which lead to violent behavior and conflicts on the surface of the episode are egoistical striving for power and appreciation, as well as suppression and exclusion of others, in other words; the strive for dominance (Dietrich 2011, 369). Dietrich mentions fear of own exclusion and domination, as well as compensation for doubts about personal social competence rooted in traumatic social experiences as reason for mistrust and consequential strive for dominance (Ibid.). Peace-work at this level is relatively complex, because imbalances and blockages in the previous structures, which are embedded in this one, also interfere and influence here. Thus, material greed (archaic) and sexual aspiration (magic) can for instance be incentives and amplifiers for the strive towards social dominance, as a higher social status in a feedback-loop enhances the prospects for material wealth and sexual partners – by which a mutually amplifying circle of potentially violence-enhancing conduct is set in motion and interferes with a harmonious flow on the contact-border of the episode. Peace-work solely focused on this layer will have to work with narratives – the personal and social mythologies – while elicitive oriented peace-work also here additionally will try to facilitate a space for consciousness raising, which moves beyond mythic rationality. Thus, the first step in transforming mythic narratives and egoistical striving is found on the next level.

2.2.4. Mental

In Gebser′s perspective the mental consciousness steps out of the concealment of the two-dimensional circle into the three-dimensional space; the necessity for a perspective. There is no being-in-the-polar-oneness anymore, only the alien opposite, the dualism, which through a mental synthesis is sought bridged as trinity (Gebser 1973, 132). It is a world of the human; in other words it is a human world, where "man is the measure of all things" (Protagoras); where human thinks self and adjust and judges (with) his/her thoughts; it is a world which is measured and objectified, a material world, which stands opposite the human. The detachment of the ego from nature is as already mentioned also an awakening of the human to itself, and a realization of itself as human, corresponding to the inscription in the Apollon-temple in Delphi: *gnothi seauton*. With this awakening the mental thinking practice gains a superior relevance, and especially so the judging thought, with which the human steps out of the hazy mythical consciousness. The human gives itself order, by stating rules and laws:

thus mediated Moses at the mountain Sinai the divine law to the people, Lykurg wrote the Spartan law, and later Solon the Athenian. With "Law" the right side gains emphasis, which does not only stand for awakened consciousness, but also for the masculine principle (Gebser 1973, 133 – 135)?

The term *mental* implies *mentality* in the sense of moral setup or mindset. Gebser traces the etymological root of *mental* to *"menos,"* which according to Gebser denotes the complex of: "*Intention, rage, courage, thinking, thought, mind, mentality, imagination*" (Ibid. 127). The basis for the mutation into the mental consciousness Gebser thus sees in "rage" and "thought," which at first is experienced mythically as "wrath of the gods," the rage of Zeus or the fury of Jahwe, but later is transferred unto the human I (Ibid.). The rage, not as blind, but as thinking rage, gives direction to reason and action. It is ruthless in the German sense of *Rücksichtslos*, which means it does not look back, but turns the human away from the preceding mythical world of enclosedness and embeddedness, and directs it forward, as the aiming spear – as Achilles plunges into the fight. The rage isolates the human from the preceding valid world – the emphasis here lies on human – and enables the I-consciousness (Cf. Ibid., 129). While the mythical reasoning was an imaginative picture conceiving, which was enclosed in the polarity-encompassing circle, the directed thought is an object-related reasoning and consequently marked by duality. The mental human sees itself as subject facing an object. Erich Neumann writes in this regard, that man in the mental consciousness always sees himself as man facing an opposite not-I. This not-I is experienced as feminine, which unconsciously associated with the Great Mother of ancient times gains demonic characteristics (Neumann 1949, 137). The Sanskrit root of mother "Ma(t)" contains terms as *matar*, from which mother and matter derive, but also meter and measure. Meter and measure belongs to the mental system, by which the masculine I seeks to dominate the mother and the matter (Ibid.). Gebser would agree with this etymological reasoning, and add that the original root "ma: me" latently and complementary also contains the feminine principle, because the Greek word for "moon," *men*, also goes back to this root, implying the association between the moon and the feminine principle. Towards the secondary root "ma(t)", Gebser notes on the same page that the contemporary patriarchal world experiences a glorification, which expresses itself in the obsession of rational man through matter and materialism. While the moon was formerly a measure for natural temporality, today matter is as measure for spatiality (Gebser 1973, 131).

One leading theme Gebser points out as characteristic for the mental stage is dualism (Ibid.). It is, however, not only the mentally realized ego-awareness that necessarily and simultaneously creates an opposite and outside "not-I," and thus the dualism between subject and object – the ego-awareness simultaneously also creates an internal dualism through its self-reflection. This is necessarily so, since the one (the ego) realizing, and the realized (the prior layers) are at least two. This dualism then, is the great source of conflict on this stage. Internally, it is the struggle Freud described as the antagonistic forces of the Id and the super-ego, which the ego has to balance. The Id corresponds here to the first three chakras (especially sexuality and emotions), while the fourth chakra in the here presented systematic creates the ego openly towards the potentials of the super-ego, while the latter especially describes the wider societal necessities and the corresponding ethical and aesthetic reasoning. Goethe expressed this split dramatically, in the famous statement *"Zwei Seelen wohnen, ach! In meiner Brust. Die eine will sich von der anderen trennen; die eine hält in derber Liebeslust, sich an die Welt mit klammernden Organen: Die andre hebt gewaltsam sich vom Dust zu den Gefilden hoher Ahnen.*[22]*"* (Goethe 1994, sentence 1112). In physiological terms, this dualism has historically been related to two different parts of the brain, on one side the limbic system which were considered responsible for the processing of emotions and drive- and instinctual behavior, and on the other hand the cerebral cortex, considered responsible for higher order reasoning and especially the ego-awareness (Bloomfield et al. 1975, 63). Arthur Koestler was of the opinion that the human urge for self-destruction, its capability of becoming addicted to drugs, and to wage wars, can be explained as a pathological split between emotions and reason, based in the imperfect coordination between those two brain-structures, which he interpreted as an error of evolution (Koestler 1967, 296).

2.2.4.1. Formal operational

In the ontogenetic consciousness-development the so-called formal operational stage corresponds to the fourth chakra, and begins at about age 11. As children/adolescents enter this stage, they gain the ability to think in an abstract manner, the ability to combine and classify items in a more sophisticated way, and the capacity for higher-order reasoning. The child can now do mathematical calculations, think creatively, use abstract reasoning, and imagine the outcome of particular actions (McLeod 2009). An example of the distinction between concrete and formal operational stages is the answer to the question "If Kelly is taller than Ali and Ali is taller than Jo, who is tallest?" This is an example of inferential reasoning, which is the ability to think about things which the child has not actually experienced, and to draw conclusions from its thinking. The child who needs to draw a picture or use objects is still in the concrete opera-

[22] Two souls live, ah! in my chest. The one seeks to free itself from the other; the one sticks in sturdy lust, to the world with clinging organs: the other elevates violently from the dust, to the realms of great forefathers." (My translation).

tional stage, whereas children who can reason the answer in their heads are using formal operational thinking.

With the ability for abstract reasoning comes the ability to reflect upon the own social role and personal conduct, as well as to emphatically place oneself in the perspective of others. The transcendence from concrete operational/mythic to formal operational/mental Wilber hence describes as a transformation from a role identity to an *ego* identity – and I could also say role-awareness to ego-awareness (Cf. Wilber 2000, 317). Again, ego (in the sense of I) does here not mean egocentric, but on the contrary it interpersonally means moving from a *sociocentric* to a *worldcentric* capacity, which means a capacity to distance oneself from one´s own egocentric and socio-centric embeddedness, and consider what would be fair for all people and not merely one´s own (Ibid.). In other words, the capacity to form concepts that go beyond the concrete episode, and enables one to have an idea about affiliations with 'imagined communities', termed society, based on abstract formulated ethical and aesthetic principles, and wider inclusion and expulsion proceedings (Cf. Dietrich 2011, 373).

2.2.4.2. Anahata

The fourth – or "heart"- chakra is called *anahata* and fits coherently with the logic of the here presented systematic, and is intra-personally related to mental activity and inter-personally to society (Cf. Dietrich 2008, 372). As Dietrich remarks, it can at first sight seem surprising that metaphorical heart qualities such as love, compassion and devotion should have something to do with mind and society (Ibid.). That this indeed makes sense already became apparent in the prior outline regarding the ontogenetic characteristics. The intra-personal capacity for mental abstraction opens up for the possibility to become aware and conscious of the personal/social role in the episode, with its sexual/energetic and family aspects, through mental self-reflection. It is this mental abstraction, which realizes the own persona and its energy – and through this, in a sense, creates the ego as further differentiation. As such, Nietzsche is right in stating that the ego is nothing but a grammatical (or rather mental) fiction, that there is no doer behind the deed. The doer is in this perspective indeed rather a fictive (mental) abstraction that *follows* the deed (in this case the abstraction) – and indeed a powerful one. At the same time that the ego stabilizes by acquiring a conscious awareness of its own constitution (archaic form, sexual energetic and social role) it also begins to *own* this constitution and can judge and correct it (at least that is the idea) (Cf. Dietrich 2011, 372). This, then, is the disruptive effect of consciousness on the vegetative psychic energetic/magic Gebser has in mind, and how the ego frees itself from magic unity and mythic polarity.

Connected to a realized ego-perspective is the potential realization that other people as well have a personal perspective, and the consequential potential to consciously try to grasp this perspective - which is called empathy. Empathy, which I understand as a prerequisite for compassion, is in regard to emotions probably only possible because of the magic/energetic unity (and correlative mirror neurons) – however, in order to not egocentrically fuse with the other or project own emotions, but exactly appreciate the other as the other, mental differentiation between I and Other is necessary[23]. This again presupposes that the personal and mental capacity actually is applied for interpersonal purposes, and thus balances the intra-personal ego-awareness. Inner ego-consciousness unbalanced by outer societal-consciousness distorts the potential heart-qualities love, compassion and devotion into power-obsession, passion and greed – through simultaneously distorting the preceding layers towards its (only then common connoted) egoistical aspects (Cf. Dietrich 2011, 374). It follows by implication that a person, who applies mental capacities for inter-personal purposes only, without self-awareness, will remain a pawn in the hands of (the then still unconscious) pre-personal collective influences.

Dietrich remarks in my view correctly that mental categories and qualities due to its dual character also always are adhesive (Dietrich 2011, 374). Love as heart-quality is inter-personally thus bound on concrete persons, while others are excluded (Ibid.). This is consequently so, since the ego as described here is a product of mental abstraction, and thus by its very nature only exist in its adhesiveness to, and identification with, its thoughts and emotions (or rather, the ego *is* the duality of thoughts and emotions) – which subsequently are set in a reflective interrelationship with other (so perceived) egos. The dualism born out of this mental process can be realized (or come into awareness) through mental reflection – however, it can logically not be solved by further mental reflection. Following the chakra-psychology of yoga, the transrational peace-philosophy thus recommend a (meditative) conscious awareness and observation of mental and emotional processes, without judging or categorizing thoughts (which would be mental), in order to transcend and integrate the mental process in an again wider and deeper understanding – which no longer is mental, but trans-mental, and the entrance to the spiritual (Ibid. 377). This particular reflection leads me straight into the next layer; however, before going there, I shall make another quick note on the term freedom.

Webster´s first definition of the adjective free is: "not bound by restrictions, physical, governmental, or moral; exempt from arbitrary domination or

[23] The circumstance that empathy to certain degrees also is found among most mammals underpins that the here described layers not have to be understood as strict categories and that all forms of human societies also had and applied mental capabilities – while I argue the different emphasize of structures according to societal organization.

distinction; independent" (Webster´s Comprehensive Dictionary 2004, 503). The meaning of this contemporary interpretation goes in a clear direction; "freedom" at this time and stage concerns the ego, its alleged individuality, and its right to unfold as an individual according to its own will, and in opposition and relation to societal necessities. In "On Liberty," John Stuart Mill sought to define the "...nature and limits of the power which can be legitimately exercised by society over the individual," and as such, he describes an inherent and continuous antagonism between liberty and authority, and thus, the prevailing political question becomes "how to make the fitting adjustment between individual independence and social control" (Mill 1869, 2). From a transrational perspective, this continuous antagonistic dualism between egoistic wants and societal needs on the one hand, and the corresponding intra-personal antagonism on the other hand is, if at all, first transcended in the next structure, where freedom intra-personally no longer denotes the freedom *of* the ego, but the freedom *from* the ego, and inter-personally encompasses a global perspective.

2.2.4.3. The Further Reaches of Human Consciousness

From here on the three models outlined by Dietrich, Gebser and Wilber cease to correlate with each other, while all three theorists continue to formulate further possible stages of consciousness.

If Wilbers next stage, "vision-logic," is disregarded as a stage of its own, because, as Wilber himself almost admits, this structure actually is a variation of the overall mental and formal operational structure (Cf. Wilber 2000, 361), then his next four transpersonal stages termed *psychic, subtle, causal* and *non-dual* do more or less correlate to the next chakras as outlined by Dietrich, which are *vishudda, anja* and *sahasrar*. The exact correlation and quantity of those stages are at this point not important, as this modeling, especially in Wilber´s case, also is a question of convention. Relevant is eventually the qualitative correlation between the last stages: non-dual and sahasrar – and their correlation to Gebser´s integral consciousness and the archaic state. Gebser, being more concerned with the phylogenetic development, identifies solely one next possible stage in relation to the preceding structures, which he termed integral consciousness, respectively a-rational or aperspectival, without implying that this should be the last possible stage of consciousness, whatsoever. However, I believe that Wilber, who correlates Gebser´s integral consciousness structure with what he terms "vision-logic," is decidedly wrong. "Vision-logic," which describes a form of post-modern globalism, is in its rationalism not at all where Gebser wanted to go. For instance, Wilber states that the academically linguistic turn would be something Gebser would approve of as further manifestation of the integral consciousness (Wilber 2000, 268). If the linguistic turn is understood as a regard of language as autonomous entity, where the signifier has nothing to do with the signified – where there even is no reality (signified) 'behind' or beyond the structuring of language – then this is definitively not where Gebser was headed, who following the principle *nomen est omen* was very interested in etymological roots in order to uncover deeper "truths" about words and circumstances, and exactly did not regard language as only reality in the constructionist sense, but intimately interwoven with reality, in line with tantric principles. Gebser points in the opposite direction from Wilber, in order to manifest the next consciousness structure. It is here, in the different evaluations of the preceding and still active structures of consciousness - the archaic, magic and mythic – that the crucial difference for this work between Gebser and Wilber is to be found. The evolutionist Wilber does not accredit these earlier structures with much validity on their own, except from being necessary, in a try-and-error fashion, to bring humanity to where it is now. Gebser on the contrary acknowledges and attest these same earlier structures much more validity, inherent coherence, and meaningfulness than Wilber. The evidence of synchronicity is in favor of Gebser´s understanding. The magic is real and mythologies woven out of real, living fabric. This has far-reaching consequences, but not necessarily decisive ones. My goal in the following is to align these different models and show how they are mutually agreeable. I believe this is possible, because Gebser´s integral consciousness indeed corresponds to Dietrich´s description of the next consciousness structure, in chakra-theory *vishudda*, which further corresponds to what Wilber terms *psychic.* What Dietrich further on describes as the sixth chakra, called *anja,* corresponds to Wilber´s *causal* while the seventh chakra, *sahasrar,* fittingly corresponds to Wilber´s description of the *non-dual.* At this point Wilber´s linear understanding of evolution moving from Alpha to Omega turns into a circular. Why and how this concretely looks, will become evident once the basic structures are outlined. In the following I will thus outline the further reaches of consciousness according to transrational peace-psychology in its reference to yogic chakra-philosophy, Gebser´s a-perspectivity and Wilber´s terminology.

2.2.5. Integral

Integral consciousness means for Gebser 'wholeness,' the restoration of the unharmed original state under the enriching implementation of all proceeding structures of consciousness. For the integral human all the prior developed structures become transparent and conscious. Also, their influences on his/her own life and fate become apparent. The deficient aspects are neutralized through insight and mastered, so that the degree of maturity and balance is achieved, which is necessary for the concretization. Concretization is the key word for

Gebser, since only the concrete can be integrated; never the abstract (Gebser 1973, 167). According to Gebser, Jacopo da Pontorm, a student of Leonardo da Vinci, made the leap from mental to integral consciousness, because in the "doctrine of the conic sections" (1639), he leaves the three-dimensional space into the fulfilled spherical globe. He thereby leaves the emptiness of the only linear space and touches upon a dimension, which as fulfillment, at least presupposes the latent presence of time (Gebser 1973, 168-169). The globe (or sphere) is then the meaningful symbol for the integral structure, since the moving globe constitutes a four-dimensional structure (Ibid.). What Gebser has in mind when he uses 'existential emptiness' as characteristic of the (mental) linear, three-dimensional space, is exactly time and the temporal emptiness of the present moment – the famous here and now - when it becomes a sole gap between past and future (Ibid. 258). It is the concretization of the moment, the here and now, which for Gebser constitutes the fourth dimension and means to make time, and the ever-present origin, concrete. Time as conscious experience manifests in the mythical structure together with the soul and for Gebser due to a reason, for him time and soul are two different terms for the same thing. Hence, when someone says, "I don´t have time," amounts to saying "I don´t have soul" (Ibid.). The temporary modern experience of a "lack of time" is for Gebser the indication that this collective stage of consciousness is in its deficient phase – with the overarching characteristic being a "ratio" which rationalizes (in the sense of dividing) time into past and future, by which the present moment is emptied and squashed into almost non-existence - and necessitates a mutation of conscious awareness.

Crucial for Gebser´s notion of integral consciousness, which he terms a-rational and a-perspectival, is that it constitutes a transparency and simultaneous diaphaneity of *all* consciousness structures - archaic, magic, mythical and mental – while the awareness of this then in itself constitutes the integral consciousness (Cf. Gebser 1973, 175). This 'mutation' has not to be understood as an *expansion* of consciousness, since this in its time and space relatedness would be a mental phenomenon, but much more as an *intensification* of consciousness – a realization of spirit – or spiritual realization. In Gebser´s own words:

> The origin is always present. It is not a beginning, since every beginning is time-bound. And the present is not just the now, the today or the moment. The present is not a piece of time, but a holistic (integral) achievement, and thus always also original. Whoever is capable, of bringing origin and present into effect and actuality as a wholeness, to realize and concretizise, he/she transcends beginning and end and just today´s time (Gebser 1973, 15, my translation).

Gebser´s strategy for transcending mental dualism and the hypertrophied ego lies thus in an integrating self-awareness. It is the diaphaneity of the whole being, which here means the preceding consciousness structures, which is brought into effect through realization and concretization, which brings origin and present into an actualized wholeness. This then is in agreement with Dietrich's outline of transrational practice and spirituality.

2.2.5.1. Vishudda

The self-reflective ability of the mental layer opens not only for the possibility of ego-consciousness, and thus for consciousness in the common sense in the first place, but in further consequence also for those desirable qualities such as compassion, love and altruism. However, the dualistic character of the ego and its adhesiveness to other egos also creates considerable problems in a peace perspective. Love is still projected on individual persons and the mythic polarities inside and outside, good and bad, true and wrong, continue to work and gain the quality of dualities. The loosening, transcendence and integration of duality and adhesiveness, which consequently is desirable (not only) in a peace-philosophical perspective, occurs in the transrational systematic on this next potential layer which I term integral, and Dietrich relates to the fifth chakra, called *Vishudda* (Dietrich 2008, 364-365). Equally, Gebser suggests transrational practice as well as self-awareness as the key to accessing this consciousness structure.

Conscious awareness and observation of mental and emotional processes, without judging or categorizing thoughts (which would be mental), can transcend and integrate the mental process in an again wider and deeper understanding – which then no longer is mental, but trans-rational and the entrance to the spiritual (Cf. Dietrich 2008, 366). The Cartesian subject, which believes to be because it thinks, and thus identifies with its thoughts, comes here to its end and is transcended and suspended in an again wider and deeper self, when the person begins to observe its thoughts and emotions (Ibid., 364). This *Internal Observer* is no longer identified with the observed thoughts and emotions, because it is *this* that observes – without reflection. What is this *this*? Safe to say, it is a part of consciousness now freed from the entrapment in thoughts and emotions. Dietrich describes this freed part of consciousness as the opening through which the deeper self can emerge from the shadows of the ego, formerly lost in thoughts and chased by emotions (Ibid., 365). Wilber calls it the soul, in reference to Emerson's notion of the Over-Soul, which here begins to shine through the opening of consciousness, no longer obscured by the ego. In this regard Wilber quotes Emerson's attempt to describe the characteristic of the soul:

> All goes to show that the soul in man is not an organ, but animates and exercises all the organs; is not a function, like the power of memory, of calculation, of comparison, but uses these as hands and feet; is not a faculty, but a light; is not the intellect or will, but the master of the intellect and the will; is the background of our being, in which they lie, - an immensity not

> possessed and that cannot be possessed. From within or from behind, a light shines through us upon things and makes us aware that we are nothing, but the light is all (Emerson, quoted after Wilber 2000, 390).

Wilber goes on explaining:

> The observer in you, the Witness in you, transcends the isolated person in you and opens instead – from within or from behind, as Emerson said – onto a vast expanse of awareness no longer obsessed with the individual bodymind, no longer a respecter or abuser of persons, no longer fascinated by the passing joys and setapart sorrows of the lonely self, but standing still in silence as an opening or clearing through which light shines, not from the world but into it... That which observes or witnesses the self, the person, is precisely to that degree free of the self, the person, and through that opening comes pouring the light and power of a Self, a Soul, that, as Emerson puts it, would make our knees bend (Ibid.).

While Wilber in this passage masterfully explains the Internal Observer and its role as gateway for the trans-personal self, it also becomes comprehensible why this is a peace-relevant development. While the light, soul, or self that Emerson, Wilber and Dietrich formulate can only be experienced personally (more correctly trans-personally), it is logically understandable that controversies and conflicts at this stage decrease dramatically. A controversy presupposes that the conflicting parties are identified with their respective stance, which reacts and fights the position of the opposition, through which those oppositions are enforced, and conflicts, which in themselves are nothing but expressions of social vitality and activity, are overcharged with energy (Dietrich 2008, 366). The Internal Observer, which no longer is identified with thoughts and emotions and consequently any position, and through this 'unconditionedness' enables the flow of unconditioned love and self, no longer forms part of this mechanism.

Dietrich remarks that what intra-personally is the Internal Observer is inter-personally the External Observer, which means the same form of detached observation only for what goes on outside the person. For peace-work this consequently means that action orientation here is transcended with detached, loving observation (Dietrich 2011, 379). This then comes close to the taoistic concept of *wuwei,* which means as much as "non-action" or "abstention from actions against the workings of nature" (Fischer 2005, 5). This does not mean to become inactive or passive, but instead of unconsciously letting the *person* act out of mental dualism, mythic power-struggle or magic emotionality, it denotes a *letting happen,* where the Soul or Self, taoistic terminology would say the *Tao*, gets its way through the person. This experience then, it seems, is also what Paul refers to when he preaches to the church in Galatia and states: "I have been crucified with Christ and I no longer live, but Christ lives in me." (Galatians 2:20). Somewhat paradoxically, the idea is that it is only from this form of non-action that genuine action can spring, while what from an ego-perspective seemed to be action at this level is unmasked as continuous reaction.

Wilber, again in reference to Emerson´s Over-Soul, would add that while internal observation allows "light to shine through" the person, external observation equally opens for the experience that the same light, the same Soul or Self, shines through everything – thus the term Over-Soul or also World-Soul (Wilber 2000, 396). Witnesses to this light-show as for instance Emerson, tell us that this is a most fulfilling and peaceful experience.

In terms of identity, the preceding mental consciousness is once again embedded in a deeper and wider identity, intra-personally the soul or self, which integrates and transcends the ego and inter-personally the same Self or World-Soul, which integrates and transcends the former abstract *idea* of globality into a direct *experience.* As a result of the detached observation and since it is one and the same deeper Self, which unconditioned shines through everything the experience is marked by non-duality. The surface on the contact-border has here become permeable or transparent ("the light shines through"), however, it is not suspended, and for the subjective experience there is more potential for being and peace present, and the goal of the yogic spiritual way is not reached yet. What Wilber here terms soul, I would like to differentiate from spirit, since I earlier mentioned that the person here is entering spiritual realms – and those two terms often are confused and used interchangeably in the debate. What follows is thus a (rather mythological) note on terminology in regard to the concepts of spirit and soul.

2.2.5.2. A Note on Spirit and Soul

It was earlier noted that the term soul in Gebser´s sense denotes *this* that awakes (to consciousness) with the mythic dream-picture production, and constitutes the symbolical (and mysterious) pre-form and background of matter and form, closely connected to meaning (intelligence) and feeling. This notion fits very well with Wilber´s and Emerson´s use of the same term, where soul denotes "the background of our being, in which they lie...". This "background" then, reminiscent of the platonic forms and Jung´s archetypes, would indeed be compatible as preform and background of matter and form, constituting a sort of global 'dream-time.' Gebser would then have to be credited for pointing out that this soul within the human awakes to consciousness in the mythological structure – and, as by now should be clear, that consciousness at this stage does not mean a reflective self-awareness, but that the consciousness is enchanted in soul – seeing the inner pictures and being in complete identity with them, while it is first with the mental capacity that it becomes possible to differentiate and integrate this identity with the soul's inner picture-production in a dualistic ego-perspective. The ego thus becomes a necessary transition stage in a further differentiation of consciousness, necessary for a wider self-awareness – or self-realization - of soul and spirit. If one regards this as a teleological process, one would possibly be labeled Hegelian – with the difference that Hegel saw mental ego-consciousness as the final expression - or self-realization - of spirit.

To differentiate between spirit and soul on this level is highly speculative and difficult, and of course also a question of convention – and eventually even unnecessary. I understand the difference to be tantric, which symbolically and mythologically speaking means to associate spirit with consciousness, the passive, contemplative principle called *Shiva,* and on the other hand the soul with the unconscious, active and energetic principle called *Shakti.* Life is in this cosmology is the interplay between those two only apparent opposites, which in the end are one – two sides of the same coin - and the reason tantric symbolism is filled with sexual allegories (Cf. Dietrich 2008, 52-53). Another allegory could be the relation between light and matter, where for instance plants only take form and bloom, as expression of life, through the meeting (or tantric mating) of light and matter – spirit and soul – while for instance plants that grow under the earth, as potatoes, are rather unshapely. But also the physical light itself shows this characteristic complementary. In the here presented systematic of the *human* development of consciousness, which in the here presented logic moves from unconsciousness to consciousness, this would simultaneously be a movement from *Shakti* to *Shiva,* from the feminine to the masculine principle, which then would have its historic correspondence in the development from matriarchy to patriarchy, while the latter presumably and fittingly sets in at the time mental consciousness became activated and dominant, and which I would place roughly at the Jasperian axis age (around 800 - 200 BC). What Gebser thus terms the awakening of the soul in mythology, or the third chakra, is in this perspective then simultaneously an awakening of spirit, albeit still enchanted in soul. Fittingly, spirit as masculine principle, which as earlier argued in the form of mental ego-consciousness at the fourth chakra, searches to dominate and subdue soul and thus interferes with the 'natural' flow of events, equivalent to a suppression of the feminine by the masculine, has now at the fifth chakra to step back (Internal/External Observer) in order to let the soul, the feminine principle, once more 'shine through.' The terms feminine and masculine as I use them here are not gender-bound, but describe cosmic principles operating (among other things) in every human, male and female alike. In as far as the here described dynamics are reflected in wider society by a stepping back of male domination superseded by equality between men and women and everything in between – and where the feminine principle is the active – this would in this perspective indeed be a welcomed development. However, where the societal developments are born out of, and moving within mental rationalism, and simultaneously are gender-bound, there can be no transformation of the basic dynamic.

Meanwhile, and without having to make associations towards gender-related concepts, it is important for the further discussion to distinguish between soul and spirit, because they imply two different understandings of the self, which otherwise will be confused. In the tradition of humanistic and later transpersonal psychology, especially where it builds on Jungian psychology, follows an understanding of the self as a central, unifying archetype, where the self is the center of the whole psyche (which does not has to be confused with the ego, which simply constitutes a reflective abstraction and is the center of that which is conscious). This particular self, I understand as equivalent with the soul, belonging to the energetic aspect of life, closely connected to form and meaning. In this understanding the self epitomizes (a pantheistic) God (or vice versa). The 'other' self, which Dietrich´s outline implies, as far as it follows Samkya-Yoga philosophy and which becomes relevant in the following structures, is described as completely attribute-less and without any relation. In Samkya Philosophy this self is called p*urusha* (Eliade 1977, 24). The only thing that can be said about *purusha* is that it is and that it apprehends (and this apprehension has to be understood as a meta-physical apprehension which roots in the contemplation of the own being) (Ibid.). This particular self, which means a pre-reflexive, conscious and subject-less being-there, I understand as equivalent with spirit.

However, before losing myself (which in the here developed sense albeit could be a great thing) in philosophical problems about mind and matter, which have been debated for at least 5000 years, I keep my above stance and suggest to understand these two selves as complementary and practically inseparable. This stance is further argued and underscored, and the more exact modalities of the relation between those two selves are outlined in the chapter on synchronicity. In spite of the inseparability of soul and spirit, what can be done is to consciously differentiate them, which is exactly what the integral describes. The Internal Observer, which I would describe as a further differentiation of spirit, enables the integration and wholesome emergence of the soul, which means nothing else than a harmonious, interrelated flow of the preceding layers.

Since spirit and soul thus are further differentiated in the integral structure, but still form a complementary pair that never comes alone, it is consequently a question of perspective which aspect one sees at the here discussed fifth chakra. Focus on the awareness will find spirit, while focus on what awareness is aware of will see and feel soul. This dualism, however, is practically solved at this stage, since awareness of having awareness, only is possible through mental reflection (ego-consciousness). 'Pure' awareness detached from mental reflection can never be aware of itself. Mystics make this point by asking: “how can a knife cut itself?” while also Wittgenstein makes the same point with his famous aphorism:

> Where *in* the world is a metaphysical subject to be noted? You say that this case is altogether like that of the eye and the field of sight. But you do *not* really see the eye. And from nothing *in the field of sight* can it be concluded that it is seen from an eye (Wittgenstein 1955, 5.633).

The observer dissolves in the observation. According to Dietrich and yogic chakra-psychology, consciousness moves from *vishudda* on to the sixth chakra, *anja*, before it is concluded in non-dual awareness at the seventh chakra, *sahasrar* (Dietrich 2008, 367). Equally, Wilber formulates further stages of consciousness – while both authors remain rather unclear on what dynamics exactly accomplish this further process. I believe one core dynamic, which causes the further movement and transformation of consciousness, is what in the literature is known as the 'burning of karma.' Karma, as I understand it, denotes an extended cause-effect principle, which not only includes the physical realm, but the psychological as well. Once consciousness is settled in observation and detached from form (archaic), feelings (magic), sociality (mythic) and thoughts (mental), karma – or psychological cause and effects – which formerly were reinforced and kept at work through identity, do now slowly come to nothing. This "burning up of karmic seeds" is practically the same process known as the ego-death, because the freedom from thoughts includes the freedom from imaginations and past memories, while the identity of the ego is constituted by memories of who this ego was in the past. When consciousness is settled in an awareness of what is real in the present, detached from thoughts and imaginations concerning the past, the ego ceases to exist (Cf. Dietrich 2008, 365). Presumably, once this process is finished, consciousness development has reached the next stage.

2.2.6. Witness-awareness

In the logic of the chakra-system the next 'stage' is called *anja.* Wilber terms this level causal, probably in reference to a divine 'first cause,' while transrational terminology here also speaks of the Witness-awareness. In reference to Krishnamurti´s interpretation of yoga-philosophy, Dietrich characterizes and differentiates the witness-awareness from the observing-awareness by its resolving of perspective (Dietrich 2011, 381). The perspective, which was gained proper in the mental structure, is dissolved in the immediate and formless awareness, which is without self, other or God. The contact-border on the surface of the episode, which became permeable in the previous stage, is here suspended. Dietrich remarks that, "through the dissolution of the contact-border the intrapersonal and interpersonal layers flow into each other in a paradoxical way" (my translation of Dietrich 2011, 382). Consequently, the formless and immediate awareness of the Witness sees not the world, because he/she is the world, and apprehends it subjectively as self-sense or self-felt and not as outer object (Ibid.). Wilber remarks in the same line that the Witness cannot be seen, for the simple reason that he is the Seer (Cf. Wittgenstein 5.633) and "the Seer itself is pure Emptiness, the pure opening or clearing in which all objects, experiences, things and events arise, but which itself merely abides" (Wilber 2000, 421). The Christian sage and mystic Eckhart von Hochheim (c. 1260 – c.

1328), better known as Meister Eckhart, describes this suspension of the contact-border, which he terms breakthrough, in following words:

> In the breakthrough, where I stand free of my own will and the will of God and of all his works and of God himself, there I am above all creatures and am neither God nor creature. Rather, I am what I was and what I shall remain now and forever. Then I receive an impulse, which shall bring me above all the angels. In this impulse I receive wealth so vast that God cannot be enough for me in all that makes him God, and with all his divine works. For in this breakthrough I discover that I and God are one. There I am what I was, and I grow neither smaller nor bigger, for I am an immovable cause that moves all things... Therefore also I am unborn, and following the way of my unborn being I can never die. Following the way of my unborn being I have always been, I am now, and shall remain eternally (Eckhart 1980, 217-218).

The experience Meister Eckhart here describes could probably also be termed the experience of Being-as-such, the ultimate peace without opposite, unborn and immovable. “It is Being-as-such which makes peace experienceable and worth striving for” (Dietrich 2011, 382). As Dietrich further remarks, and in consequence with the here applied logic of consciousness development so far, this Being pervades and comprises all the prior described layers, from the surface of the episode to the mental and spiritual levels – and thus gives meaning to peace-work on the pre-egoic and egoic levels and beyond (Ibid.). Important for my work to note is that 'meaning' or 'significance' (in German one would say “*Sinn*”) is a category only relevant on the prior discussed consciousness structures – from the archaic to the integral – while meaning is meaningless in the non-dual Being of the Witness. Meister Eckhart again:

> It is free of all names and barren of all forms, totally free and void, just as God is void and free in himself. It is totally one and simple, just as God is one and simple, so that we can in no manner gaze upon it (Eckhart 1980, 294).

Meaning as a meaningful category is subject to duality and presupposes something meaningless, while in the non-dual immediate and formless Being, free of all names and void, there is no meaning or significance, as Eckhart says, it is simple and one - the famous all-one. This circumstance shall be a guiding point when accessing synchronicity, where 'meaning' is a decisive factor.

2.2.7. Non-dual

On a first glance Wilber and Dietrich diverges from each other in the assessment of what lies beyond the witness-awareness. For Dietrich, as pointed out, the witness describes non-dual awareness, Being-as-such without difference, basically indescribable, since every description necessitates a perceiving subject and an objectifying language – exactly what the witness-awareness is not (Dietrich 2011, 383). Awareness is, simple and one, without illusions or constructions. Hence, beyond the global witness-awareness vanishes not only the subject with its borders, but also Being-as-such. What Dietrich in reference to Lederach terms the epicenter means accordingly the Nothing, the Emptiness or void, which stands behind Being (Ibid.). If one might assume that Nothing not only stands behind Being, but also before – meaning that original Being springs from Nothing - then a circle is closed and Being can once more spring from Nothing. This is just about what Wilber formulates. According to Wilber, what lies beyond the Witness-awareness is not Nothing, but the rise of a new universal (awareness), which he now in turn terms *non-dual.* The move from what Wilber calls causal (the Witness-awareness) to what he calls non-dual he sees reflected in the old Shankara quote:

> The world is illusory;
> Brahman alone is Real;
> Brahman is the world.

The first two lines represent in Wilbers reading causal, e.g. Witness awareness, or unmanifest absorption in formless Spirit (Wilber 2000, 418). "The world is illusory; Brahman alone is Real" means thus that everything seen is object, ephemeral, symbol or vision – which is exactly what the Seer is not, but as Brahman, the Witness as formless awareness, Being-as-such alone is real. The third line, according to Wilber, describes in a further movement the ultimate completion, the union of the Formless with the entire world of Form (Ibid.). In Wilber´s words:

> When one breaks through the causal absorption in pure unmanifest and unborn Spirit, the entire manifest world (or worlds) arises once again, but this time as a perfect expression of Spirit and as Spirit. The Formless and the entire world of manifest Form – pure Emptiness and the whole Kosmos – are seen to be not-two (or non-dual). The Witness is seen to be everything that is witnessed, so that… the object to be witnessed and the Witness finally merge together and Absolute consciousness alone reigns supreme… This non-dual consciousness is not other to the world: "Brahman is the World" (Ibid.).

When the ego died in the previous stages, here something is reborn. Once again, I-World-God are one, or rather, there is no I, World or God – only Being. As Wilber points out, this "state" is the ultimate *decentering* of the Self – the end of all egocentrism, sociocentrism, worldcentrism etc. (Ibid. 428). Confined to nothing it embraces everything. Whether this description of Wilber not only sounds like, but also means exactly the same as Dietrich´s description of the prior Witness-awareness, and thus constitutes a flawed differentiation, or whether it is a rightfully observed further development beyond the Witness before an eventual epicenter in Nothingness – or whether Dietrich is 'wrong' and beyond the Witness is not Nothing, but an even greater merging of Being and Nothing as Wilber then correctly would state – is an interesting, albeit not relevant question, since both authors agree on the fundamental circumstances. Ultimate, experienceable or apprehensible reality, and here such superlatives seem allowed, is non-dual and characterized by the All-One. These terms are revealing. Why not simply one – but always non-dual or not-two? The mystical authors of old and new seem unable to completely let go of ambiguity. Not-two means not One either. Also the All-One is ambiguous, when the all in its great gathering and cuddling gets quite all-one. This rest of ambiguity, somewhere between one and not-two, seems to be a basic voltage necessary for life – where there is something, there is also something more. If someone ever should get beyond this ambiguity, he or she will probably not be able to come back and tell about it. Then, non-duality seems indeed the deepest truth about life expressible. From the highest spiritual insight, non-duality, when the Witness is seen to be everything that is witnessed, it derives that there must be perfect correspondence between inner and outer world, above and below, Witness and witnessed. This principle of correspondence has probably been the guiding line for philosophy and cosmology, and every thereby guided activity for the greatest period of human written history. Through 'underground' practice in the so-called Western world, first with the alchemical and hermetic traditions – in opposition to the Christian church – such thinking was introduced. In this particular line of succession it dates back to the famous *tabula smaragdina* ascribed to the mythic Hermes Trismegistos, who allegedly was a fellow of Moses, but more likely was written in Alexandria around 6th to 8th Century by Arabic magicians[24]. In Isaac Newton´s translation the second paragraph of the tabula reads: "That which is below is like that which is above & that which is above is like that which is below to do the miracles of one only thing"[25]. This principle was long before Newton not only the guideline for a great spirit like Paracelsus, but is for instance also the principle underlying astrology and all sorts of divination in general. Hence, when transrational peace-study takes this principle on board again, this is not a new science at all, but means to tie in where the thread was lost, roughly at the end of the Renaissance. The avant-garde and hyper-modern sounding term 'transrational peace-philosophy' reveals itself thus as a sort of neo-conservative renaissance, a label which also Jung could claim, as soon shall become evident.

---

[24] As such its appearance coincide time-wise with the emerging of tantrism in the northern parts of India.

[25] Source: http://www.sacred-texts.com/alc/emerald.htm retrieved latest 25.03. 2015.

2.2.7.1. The Principle of Correspondence

Before finishing this first part of the thesis and turning to Jung´s work, I shall make two points, where the first is a quick remark concerning the relation between synchronicity and the principle of correspondence, and in further consequence non-duality. The point is that synchronicity also can be defined in terms of correspondence. Synchronicity, as Jung used the term and I as well use it, is an umbrella term for all instances of seemingly *meaningful* coincidence, correlation or *correspondence* between an inner psychic event and an outer event – in other words observer and observed – not connected by any known causal chains. The term 'meaning' has here the double function of both constituting the reference axis, meaning that a correspondence in meaning connects the two causally unrelated events or processes, and in later consequence as well in the sense of 'intention' somehow literally establishing the connection in the first place, by which random events of coincidence are ruled out (Jung considered the archetypes responsible for synchronistic events). A banal example is to think of an old friend the minute before the phone rings and the friend is giving a call. This could be a random, in other words meaningless, coincidence, but it could also be a decent instance of synchronicity organized by a transpersonal agency – as for instance the intention of the friend. However, when the Seer and the Seen are one, as allegedly is the case for the Witness or non-dual awareness, when *the intrapersonal and interpersonal layers flow into each other in a paradoxical way,* then this is a full-blown synchronistic experience (Cf. Surprise 2012, 105). A subtle point to be made here, though, is that for the Witness or non-dual awareness, this is *not* experienced as synchronicity, since the experience of synchronicity presupposes an analytic mind (an awareness separating inner and outer and thus an awareness marked by duality) in order to see the coincidence of inner and outer, which the Witness exactly does not. This is a paradox equal to the saint, who stops being a saint the moment he/she realizes that he/she is a saint. This is a relevant observation, when later placing the experience of synchronicity within the here outlined development of consciousness.

A last point in this part of the writing concerns the relation and structural correspondence, respectively differences, between the first and the last layers of consciousness development, here especially some profound resemblances between archaic and non-dual awareness. Hence, in the following I will sum up the discussion so far, and discuss the resemblance respectively between the first and the last consciousness structure, and in this way finish up this part of the thesis.

2.3. On the Correlation of the First and the Last Layers

The spectrum of consciousness from archaic to non-dual as here outlined is described as a continuous, or in Gebser´s terms erratic, movement and increase in consciousness, from un-conscious instinct-based agency in the archaic state to, seen from a mental perspective, a form of super-consciousness or pure awareness in the non-dual. Another characteristic is the continuous (or erratic) widening and decentering (universalization) of the personal reference frame. From the archaic, which is characterized by a pre-personal and unconscious self-world fusion, where self and the immediate seen and experienced world are one (egocentric), to the (less) egocentric reference frame of the magic consciousness (family) to the sociocentrism of the mythic stage (tribe/community), ethic world-centrism on the mental stage (society), global reference at the integral (Policy) to the planetary reference of the Witness (global) and the final, conscious fusion of Seer and Seen, subject and object, where the personal Self dissolves and one spontaneously and synchronistic partakes as expression of the All-One (Universal).

This decentering and widening of the frame of reference is counterbalanced by a particularization and individualization (individuation) of the selfunderstanding/knowledge or identity - in other words a deeper within. The archaic consciousness lives thus by instinctual agency and in pre-personal identity fusion with the episode on the surface of the contact border (physical self-physical world identity). Magic consciousness has differentiated the physical self from the physical world, living in emotional identity with the surrounding/collective. At the mythic stage are feelings and emotions differentiated and organized into complex mythological systems and the identity is here with the social role. First at the mental layer with its reflexive abilities, a stable ego-awareness can develop, which integrates and is mentally aware of its physical surroundings, feelings, emotions and its social role - and is in identity with its dualistic mental self-image. From here the transpersonal sphere opens up, where the mental ego-identity is integrated and transcended in an integral awareness or observation, by which the again deeper self or soul comes to the fore as the new center of identity and conscious experience. What is this self or soul? Consistent with the logic of this outline would be to describe the self as an again wider frame in which the whole person together with the mental ego-perspective is included and integrated. In Jungian terms, it is the organizing center for the whole psyche, which always already was there, but operated in the unconscious. Consistent with Gebser´s argument is also to assume, that it is the same self or soul which awoke to dream-like consciousness in the mythic structure, and gave rise to the worlds mythologies, albeit, in terms of consciousness, in enchanted fusion and identity, and not as the self-conscious state of the integral. If it is the same self, or in Emerson´s terms the same World-Soul, which expressed itself unconsciously and intuitively in the mythic structure, and now once again comes to the fore, and due to the meanwhile gained and integrated ego-consciousness this time as self-conscious structure, then this is agreeing with the transrational peace-philosophy´s self-description as consciously taking *energetic* (here differentiated into archaic, magic and mythic) notions of peace on board again, without thereby renouncing rationality or *mental* achievements such as ego, democracy or human rights (Cf. Dietrich 2011, 14). This arguably being the case, I could add the description 'trans-mythic' to the term integral, and thereby point to its relation with the mythic structure, of which the integral structure arguably looks like a conscious mirror image. Following this logic, it shows that the next layer, the global Witness-awareness, indeed can be described as 'trans-magic.' The self as soul is here transcended. In terms of going within,' one could probably also say that the self here has been followed to its source – arriving at the famous Being-as-such. As mentioned, it is the magic structure characterized by its rather egalitarian pre-personal and pre-temporal frame of reference, where processes in the episode are linked in immediate meaningful or magic (Jung would say synchronistic) relations to various present agents, which consequently stand in a meaningful (symbolical) and immediate, contrary to a causal, relation with each other. The power to magically/synchronistically 'cause' events can reside in the various present agents (witchcraft - which can be conducted by both visible and invisible entities). The move from magic to mythic means simultaneously the move from a rather flat structure to a more hierarchical structure, where the magical power is transferred from humans and animals to higher order gods and goddesses, where for instance the collapse of a roof or a bad harvest no longer is ascribed to the ill will of the neighbor, but to the ill will of a fellow god/goddess. The step from the integral to the Witness-awareness now has structural analogousness to the step from magic to mythic, just in reverse: while at the trans-mythic integral structure a god-image like self is at the fore, the 'trans-magic' Witness is characterized not by *pre*-personal but by *trans*-personal and *trans*-temporal (the famous here and now) *Self-less-ness.* That is because for the magic consciousness, just as for the formless awareness of the Witness, there exists no self, other or God. What for the magic structure is a hazy point-like unity seems for the Witness to be clear global oneness, while the "paradoxical flowing into each other of intrapersonal and interpersonal layers" is a fitting description of both states from a rational perspective. This, however, does not mean that the two states at any rate are the same, while pre-personal and trans-personal also mean two widely different things. Magic and trans-magic seem, if at all, complete inversions of each other. Of the Witness awareness it is said that it sees not the world, because it *is* the world; while of the magic consciousness it can be said it sees not the world, because it is scattered all over the world. The difference is similar to whether one is riding or getting ridden, or whether one is a mother nurturing its child, or one is a child nurtured by the mother (and while at the picture, remember that the modern/mental stage structurally corresponds to an adolescent, typically believing not to need the parents and living in rebellion against them - while 'them' here means the system called world). More concretely, the Witness awareness has merged with the spirit of the planet (or even the planetary system) and when he/she moves, he/she moves as one with the whole system, which is why there is no other. Magic consciousness on the contrary, in its pre-personal inability to stand against the wider collective mind, is moved and often chased by these wider, transpersonal minds. This is at least how I read the respective passages. The evidence from both the magic structure as well as the Witness shows, that we are all one at a certain depth, and instantly connected and influencing the all locally and globally via our thoughts and emotions. The difference is whether we in magic pre-personality are owned and ruled by every hunch of thoughts and emotions, or in trans-personal awareness have taken responsibility and balancing ownership. However different they are, I believe these two states are united in the circumstance that they relate to, and respectively express, the same all-oneness. This leads me to the final within, which is the final beyond – the ultimate Omega point termed the epicenter, and its relation to the Alpha point in consciousness termed archaic.

On a first glance could it seem that these two Alpha and Omega points could not be more different; the one described as complete unconsciousness and the other as ultimate consciousness. However, the similarities they share in their respective descriptions, are in many ways also the greatest, which probably is why they often are confused or taken for the same – in one direction or the other. Hence, there are two general fallacies: one where both pre- and trans-personal experiences are understood as pre-personal states, and conversely one where every non-rational state of consciousness is understood as trans-rational (Wilber 1993, 125). The demarcation-line for Wilber, whether something is trans-personal or pre-personal, depends on whether the experience is a personal plus (integrating) – or a personal minus (resolution) (Wilber 2000, 389). The modern, scientific world has most of the time interpreted every kind of non-personal experience as regresses into infantile and schizoid states of consciousness, as for instance Freud, who explained trans-personal experiences as prenatal id-impulses and trans-subject/object Samadhi (Witness-awareness) as a regress to pre-subjective/objective-narcissism, while he interpreted trans-personal unity as pre-personal fusion (Wilber 2000, 179). In this Freudian view, which also is the orthodox and general scientific outlook, the normal ego-consciousness constitutes the peak of evolution, the end of history, and every other state of consciousness is consequently of inferior nature.

Conversely, the second type of fallacy elevates pre-personal experiences to transpersonal and does in the end see the cosmic development moving from some spiritual heights down to a culmination in a low point of self-alienation, the 'sinful' human, or the individual and personal ego (Wilber 1993, 125). God and nature, respectively spirit and nature, are seen as identical, and the respective states of consciousness always superior to ego-consciousness. Exemplary are for Wilber the 'New Age movement' (whatever he specifically might have in mind by this rather broad term) and Jung (Wilber 2000, 291). Jung does, according to Wilber, often confuse pre-personal states with trans-personal, as when he interprets the infantile narcissism as an unconscious slumbering in the *unio mystico* (Wilber 2000, 290). The Jungian scholar Erich Neumann indeed made substantial corrections on the Freudian narcissism-concept. Freud´s so called primary narcissism, which is his description of the archaic state, and where he formulates an intrauterine primal state of symbiotic fusion between an absolute pleasure-ego with its surroundings, is for Neumann a primal *"Sein in der Einheitswirklichkeit"*[26], the total *participation mystique* in which the self is all and all is the self, beyond a first later to be developed subject/object duality (Neumann 1955, 4). This phase termed Neumann *uroboric*, which is not - as Freud´s doctrine supposed – devoid of relationship because it is devoid of any object, but as a *primary relation* of the child to the mother, it is the basis of further development. Neumann further remarks that Freud´s nomination of this primary narcissism as being autoerotic is also misguiding for this phase. The objectless self-love could indeed be interpreted as autoerotic, however, if one wants to speak about objectless self-love one also has to speak about subject-less all-love as well as of a subject/object-less all-being-loved (Ibid. 5). Clearly, Neumann following Jung does not only do justice to the unborn infant, but by implication also describes the archaic state as an unconscious form of pre-subject/object Samadhi. Hence, Wilber, who as seen earlier in regard to the archaic is in line with Freud, laments that Jung and his followers do not understand development moving from unconscious pre-personal to personal to conscious trans-personal, but rather from unconscious trans-personal to personal to conscious trans-personal (Wilber 1993, 128). I agree with Wilber´s assessment that Jungians tend to see development moving from unconscious slumbering in the self to the ego (this is understood as extrovert 'initiation into the outside world' and belonging to the first half of the life) and then back again to the self (in Jungian terminology the introspective 'initiation into the inside world' belonging to the second half of life – while the latter process also is called individuation) (Cf. Jacobi 1971, 129). That they thereby theoretically often confuse mythic and magic aspects with integral and trans-personal modalities, as well as the direction of development – seen from a transrational perspective – is not a logical consequence, however, as I shall argue, Jung and Jungian psychology practically often move toward pre-personal resolution as Wilber claims, especially when it comes to synchronicity. At the same time I agree with Jung and his successors that the archaic state in fact constitutes an unconscious slumbering in the All-One, which means that Wilber´s linear understanding of

[26] In English: Being in the reality of Oneness. My translation.

evolution rather has to be seen as circular when it comes to spirituality. Exactly because pre-modern and pre-rational societies were and are highly spiritual can a trans-rational approach twist their wisdom and take up the thread of spirituality, and transcend the contradictions of the modern age without giving up its achievements (Cf. Dietrich 2011, 14).

2.3.1. Closing the Circle

Following the tantric principle of *Shiva* and *Shakti*, where *Shakti* stands for the unconscious, active energetic principle and Shiva for the conscious, contemplating principle, both being two aspects of a non-dual oneness, I propose, in order to settle this conflict between the Jungian school and Wilber´s rather Freudian inspired outlook, to understand the primal archaic state and the non-dual awareness as corresponding to, or even 'embodying,' these principles. Obviously, the archaic state then relates to *Shakti,* while the non-dual awareness relates to *Shiva*, while both Alpha and Omega points simply are two different aspects of the same original Being-as-such, by which any difference in value is excluded. To completely close this mythological circle, it should be added that in tantric philosophy the world is born from the mating of *Shiva* and *Shakti* (Alpha point), while the ultimate spiritual goal (Omega) is to realize this unification once again in the here termed non-dual epicenter, the background of Being, which in terms of sex would be androgyny (the unification of *Shiva* and *Shakti*) and in the transrational understanding equivalent to peace. "I am the Alpha and the Omega," says the Lord God, "who is, and who was, and who is to come, the Almighty." (Revelation 1:8)[27]. Thus having arguably given in to the Jungian interpretation, I also have to agree with Wilber, that the direction of development cannot be confused. There are worlds apart between integrating and transcending the physical, ego and self, and growing into a trans-personal awareness of the All-One on the one hand – and consciously trying to regress back into the pre-personal helpless peace of the motherly womb, which however, was not what Jung and his followers sought to do.

[27] That there actually are two epicenters and that this is of central importance has recently also been introduced into the transrational discourse (Cf. Dietrich 2015, 43 and 47-48).

3. Jung and Synchronicity

There is one common flow,
one common breathing,
all things are in sympathy.
(Hippocrates)[28]

In this chapter I will relate and discuss the Jungian concept of synchronicity in light of the earlier developed theoretical framework. It will become evident how Jung developed an *energetic* worldview, moving from mythic to magic, especially due to his experiences with synchronicity, and in a paradoxical move in a certain sense issued forth to the integral structure, by working on the mythical and magical levels. It will further become evident how his findings and conclusions in regard to synchronicity were groundbreaking, as they were bringing Jung close to the all-one and the inner workings of the larger systemic minds. However, as I will argue, his synchronicity-concept has to be taken with caution from a trans-rational perspective, since it is not exactly trans-rational, but moves within a mythic frame of reference and mode of consciousness. This means, I do not reject Jung´s argument, but attest it validity within its own confines and acknowledge that to a certain degree for instance some forms of divination might be applicable for transrational peace-work, as they did and do within *energetic* frames of reference. However, as a general mode of consciousness and frame of reference, such as Jung developed for himself, the synchronistic perspective is problematic in a peace perspective due to its egocentrism and adherence to mythic consciousness. What this exactly means will become evident in the following.

In the following I will begin with a rather general introduction into the topic of synchronicity as conceptualized by Jung and his followers. When outlining Jung´s psychology, I will already discuss it in light of the extended diagram of Transrational Peace, before placing and discussing the synchronicity-concept in a transrational peace-perspective.

[28] Cited after Combs and Holland 1996, xxii.

3.1. Re-discovering an ancient Principle

At the core of the transrational perspective and elicitive method dwells the *energetic* and post-modern insight that “there are no things but only networks and interrelations. The universe is an interwoven net of connectivity,” while “in nature, no static structure exist,” and thus, “peaces are a dynamic equilibrium” (Dietrich 2011, 14). In an interconnected universe, every action has *a priori* consequences for the whole universe and everyone is hence compelled to take the whole universe into consideration, when attempting to act peacefully and ethically responsibly. Kant´s categorical imperative is here transformed to an absolute imperative and the challenge is seemingly impossible. I am requested to act as if I in every instance could know, what I have to do, as soon as I understand myself as agent in the network of networks. Every instance I have to gross up the effects of my actions on the ecology of the whole universe. I have to stand my ground as a universal citizen, while I barely know my neighbors, neglect my friends and already are overcharged with my own nation. I am asked to develop into a fakir of co-existence with everyone and everything, and ideally reduce my footprint in the environment to the trace of a feather. In the light of this challenge, the question arises, whether “universe” constitutes an encounter-able entity and has a valid address? As outlined above the transrational answer is “yes.” Through meditative practice and observation I can develop consciousness and might eventually link into global, planetary and cosmic minds – and that those encounters are characterized as experiences of the most profound peace has been witnessed by mystical traditions of all times and regions (Dietrich 2008, 374). However, what am I as spiritual layman to do, when in dire need of hints from the universe regarding what direction of action is in accordance with the greater harmony?

The classical answer to this need has been to consult an oracle or otherwise look for signs and omens in the environment. This practice, in different variations found in all cultures at all times – and in premature hubris discarded as superstitious nonsense by the enlightened modern man – builds in the end on observations and ontological assumptions familiar to the transrational philosophy. This is not strange, since the transrational philosophy is exactly characterized by its conscious integration of the pre-modern, energetic worldview(s), where the oracular inquiry and regard for signs and omens in nature played such an essential role. The Shang dynasty for instance, which traditionally is described as the second dynasty in Chinese history, and ruled China from around the 16th century BC until the 11th century BC, was the first Chinese dynasty to bequeath written testaments to the posterity, and distinguish-hed itself by its sophisticated agriculture, pottery and constructions – and con-stitutes a society completely build on oracle enquiry. At the height of the Shang-time the emperor questioned the tortoise-bone oracle about everything; from campaigns, weather, hunting, building projects to administrative instructions, dreams, the children of concubines and toothaches. Every day the emperor would attend the oracle with an enquiry, which took several hours (Peat 1987, 150-151). Invading Zhou warriors, who initiated the third dynasty in Chinese history, eventually overran the Shang-dynasty. The tortoise-bone oracle survived and is still practiced to this day in China, but was replaced as the central oracle by an equally old, but more portable method of divination, known as the *I Ging.*

Known in Europe since the 17th century CE, due to a partial translation by Richard Couplet, among others the last great polymath Gottfried Wilhelm Leibniz prized the *I Ging* highly, and saw his invention of the binary number system anticipated in it (Mungello 1999, 59-60). However, it was first with the groundbreaking translation in 1923 by the German Sinologist Richard Wilhelm that the *I Ging* found a wider reception in Europe. With the death of Richard Wilhelm in 1930 begins the modern history of academic inquiry into the workings of divination, since it was at Wilhelm's funeral that the depth-psychologist Carl Gustav Jung in his obituary to his friend Wilhelm for the first time publicly used the term *synchronistic principle* as the hypothetical principle on which he believed the working of the *I Ging* rests[29].

Jung, who had engaged himself deeply with the *I Ging* during one summer, had found the results which the oracle enquiry produced most stunning, and valued the book as a priceless entry into the unconscious – seeing the 64 hexagrams of the *I Ging* depicting the play of the archetypes (Franz 1974, 11). Later, in his 1951 foreword to Cary F. Barnes English translation of Wilhelm's German version of the I Ging, Jung briefly extrapolates his synchronicity-principle. There, Jung proposes that the Chinese mind, as it expresses itself in the *I Ging*, is exclusively occupied with the chance aspect of things, contrary to the causal aspects, which pass rather unnoticed (Jung 1950, 591). Anticipating Fritjof Capra by about 20 years, Jung notes that the ancient Chinese mind contemplates the cosmos comparably to modern physicists, who cannot deny that their model of the world is a decidedly psychophysical structure, where microphysical events include the observer - just as much as the reality underlying the *I Ging* comprises subjective, i.e., psychic conditions in the totality of the momentary situation (Ibid. 592). Whoever invented the *I Ging* was convinced that the hexagram worked out in a certain moment coincided with the latter in quality and time, and the hexagram thus was an exponent of the moment it was cast, indicating the essential situation prevailing in the moment of its origin[30]. In other words, the idea is a *correspondence* between the inner and the outer world. The curious principle underlying this assumption is what Jung

---

29 Published in Jung's foreword to Cary F. Barnes english translation of Richard Wilhelm's German translation of *The Secret of the Golden Flower.* Harcourt, Brace & World, 1962, pp. 138 – 140.

30 The *I Ging* works by either tossing coins or drawing yarrow stalks in a way that one ends up with six different lines, which then forms a certain hexagram out of 64 possible results, conforming to a corresponding interpretation in the *I Ging*.

termed *synchronicity* (Cf. Ibid.). Just as causality describes the sequence of events, so synchronicity in Jung´s view deals with the coincidence of events. For illustration: the causal point of view tells a dramatic story of how *D* came into existence: it took its origin from *C,* which existed before *D* and in its turn has a father *B,* etc. The synchronistic point of view on the other hand deals with the equally meaningful picture of coincidence; how does it happen that *A´, B´, C´,D´,* etc. all appear in the same moment and in the same place? Jung´s synchronistic answer is; it happens in the first place because the physical events *A´*and *B´*are of the same quality as the psychic events *C´* and *D´* (inseparability of observer and observed), and further because all are the exponents of one and the same momentary situation (Ibid; xxv). In other words, the external events reflect the inner-psychic events, and there is arguably a paradoxical flowing into each other of the intra-personal and inter-personal layers. The situation itself is assumed to represent a readable or understandable picture – in transrational terminology one would say *Gestalt.* In many ways Jung did with these considerations develop a sort of *systemic* reasoning equal to, and at about the same time as Ludwig van Bertalanffy developed his "General System Theory" (1949). Observer and observed (the *whole* situation and not just a single object) are considered intrinsically connected in a larger pattern – Bertalanffy would probably say ecology or *system*[31]. As an over-simplified example, take for instance an ideal-typical situation on the savanna: the wildebeest and antelopes are grazing peacefully, the baboons are roaming and looking under stones, and the birds are fighting and mating in the acacias while a pride of lions is dazing openly in the sun. Suddenly, when two of the lionesses get up for hunting, the whole scenery changes; a vigilante bird gives a warning call to the frustration of the lionesses - the call is heard and understood by the baboons who now stop and listen vigilantly, this again is seen by the antelopes who stop up alerted, etc. The intent of the lionesses, due to the correct interpretation of the bird, spreads like a wave through the scenery and seen from the lionesses perspective comes back as feedback-loop, forcing the lionesses to stalk much more carefully now, if they want any chance for success. Maybe the nervous antelopes start running even before an attack is launched, which will trigger the flight instinct in the other animals as well – and this *Gestalt* fades dramatically away and a new scenery begins to build up, once the lions unsuccessfully lay down once more, waiting until even stronger hunger makes them go on the hunt again. I am aware that system-theoretical and especially ecological considerations normally have rather bigger movements as object, as for instance too many lions might kill too many zebras – however, once the zebra population has shrunk, there is not enough

31 It has to be noted that these considerations presumably never entered a Chinese mind, for whom according to old tradition it are „spiritual agencies" making the yarrow stalks give meaningful answers (Jung 1950, 593).

game for the lions, which consequently will shrink the lion population, by which the zebra population can grow again, etc. until a *Fließgleichgewicht* (dynamic equilibrium, my translation) is established. I believe, however, that system-theoretical considerations apply at most levels, and also at more immediate situations, as in the above example. Nevertheless, there are essential differences between general *system theory* and synchronicity. In the above savanna-example, all agents acted and reacted unto each other and formed a (more or less harmonious) whole. All actions, however, where standing in, or at least can be described as, a causal interrelationship with each other – just as the earlier described correspondences between for instance the intra-personal layer of sexuality and the inter-personal layer of the family stand in a causal interrelationship as described by Dietrich (Cf. Dietrich 2015, 51). The distinguishing feature of synchronicities on the other hand is, that the interrelationship between the different involved events is not causal – or at least not stands in any known or easily imaginable causality – as for instance when the pattern of randomly tossed coins relates meaningfully and simultaneous to the wider situation of the coin tosser. Hence, the term synchronicity denotes *acausal* connections.

3.1.1. ESP and Synchronicity

In his 1952 published treatise on the subject of synchronicity, called "Synchronizitaet als ein Prinzip akausaler Zusammenhänge" Jung proposes synchronicity as a principle equal in rank and complementary to causality. What brought Jung to such a drastic proposition was accumulated experience with phenomena he felt had major importance for his own work and life – and was something he could not neglect in spite of the academic pitfalls he would face when writing on the subject[32]. Since he was aware that simply anecdotal evidence would not be convincing for the critical and academic public, he based his exposition/theorizing on the work of J. B. Rhine, who at Duke University experimentally and scientifically inquired soundly into the para-psychological topic of extra-sensory perception (ESP). ESP means the ability to perceive without using the common five senses (as for instance in pre-cognitive dreams or as clairvoyants claim to do), hence the term "extra-sensory perception." The simple experiment set-up Rhine and his colleagues used is basically composed of an experimenter, who uncovers a series of cards holding numbers and simple geometrical figures, one card at the time. Simultaneously a test subject, who is

[32] The phenomena Jung experienced himself are equal to my own experiences described in the introduction.

spatially divided from the experimenter, is given the task to tell the corresponding figures on the uncovered cards. There were used a set of 25 cards, consisting of always five cards holding the same sign. Five cards were marked by a star, five by a rectangle, five by a circle, five cards where marked by two wave-lines and five by a cross. The cards were shuffled mechanically by a machine so that the experimenter who uncovered did not know what cards he were uncovering, while the test subject placed in a different room had no chance to see the cards and had to guess or intuit the uncovered cards as well as possible. Many test runs were negative, which means that the results of the test subject did not exceed the chance probability of five correct guesses. The results of certain test subjects, however, exceeded the chance probability significantly. The first test run consisted in every test subject trying eight hundred times to guess a card. The average result of all test subjects were 6,5 correct out of 25, which means 1,5 more than the mathematical probability. The probability of a deviation of 1,5 from five is 1:250000 (Jung 1990, 21). This means that the deviation of 1,5 is likely to happen only once in 250000 cases - while it here is the unlikely average in every case (Rhine 1956, 35). Much more significant and interesting, however, were the test results of certain gifted individuals. A young man for instance, who in many tests got an average score of 10 correct out of 25, once read all 25 cards correctly, which is a performance that makes is absurd to count in probability (Ibid. 36). While these only are a few numbers of the achieved results, J. B. Rhine, who initially had set out to debunk spiritualists and other clairvoyants, concludes that the overall results were "so significant by mathematical measurements as to leave no doubt that something beyond chance was occurring in the experiment." (Ibid.)[33]. This experiments were later also conducted with increased physical distance between the experimenter and the test subject, in one case 350 kilometers, with equal results (Jung 1990, 21). With the help of synchronized watches there were also conducted experiments between Durham in North Carolina and Zagreb in Yugoslavia (around 5600 km) with equally positive results (Cited after Jung 1990, 22). Another well-documented (albeit non-experimental) case, suggesting that space is no hindrance in the minds ability to perceive things without use of the recognized senses, is the famous "Swedenborg fire," related by Immanuel Kant in his book on Emanuel Swedenborg. While in Göteborg in 1759 Swedenborg described a fire occurring in Stockholm about 480 kilometers away. He gave an account of the fire to the city authorities, naming the owner of the house that was burned, and when the fire was put out. Several days later a royal messenger arrived and confirmed the accuracy of the clairvoyant vision (Rhine 1956, 47).

---

[33] For other substantial research in the same area with equal positive results, see for instance; Tyrell, G. N. M. (1938): „Science and Psychical Phenomena", Tischner, Rudolph (1925): „Telepathy and Clairvoyance" or Humbphrey, Betty (1945): „Handbook of Tests in Para-psychology".

Even more strange is that *time* seems to not be a hindrance for ESP, because the 'reading' of cards which only are to be uncovered in the future show equal positive results beyond statistical probability (Ibid. 61). I agree with Jung´s deduction that these circumstances, that *space* and *time* in principle has no effect on the results of ESP experiments, proof that the phenomena cannot be explained by force- or energy transmission, since increased space otherwise should have a lowering effect on the results – while it becomes almost absurd and impossible to imagine an energy transmission from the future back to the present moment. This means that a causal explanation for these phenomena is virtually impossible, since causality requires the existence of space and time, because all observations in a causal perspective in the end are based on moving bodies (Jung 1990, 22). Space and time, however, seem practically relative to the mind, or in certain psychic conditions reducible to zero.

Worth mentioning are also those tests conducted by Rhine who inquire into psychokinesis (PK), which means the ability to influence matter with the mind/psyche. In these tests the test subject is given the task to cast dices (which is done by a machine) with the aim to get as many threes as possible, for instance. The results of these tests were also positive, and the more so, the more dices there were used at once (Rhine 1956, 73-75). That the moving body should be relative to the psyche is only consequent, when space and time are as well.

An experience made with all those experiments is the circumstance that the hit ratio begins to decline after the first run, and that the results from then on start to be negative, unless for some reason the interest and engagement of the test person heightens again, in which case the hit ratio rises as well. This means that indifference and boredom are inhibiting; while participation, positive expectation, hope and faith in the possibility of ESP and PK improve the results – and thus seem to be conditions for the emergence of the phenomena in the first place (Cf. Jung 1990, 23).

There have of course been great efforts to disprove these results, which border on the unbelievable and miraculous - and raise serious questions about the common worldview and well-established academic paradigms. However, these efforts all failed, and the results have presently not been refuted. Through Rhine´s experiments we are confronted with the scientifically established fact, that there exist events which stand in meaningful connection with each other, without this connection being of any known or even imaginable causal nature, since it is impossible to point out how or where the energy transmission should take place.

Rhine´s experiments are not the only area in science where unbelievable dynamics are witnessed. In quantum physics a variety of strange phenomena have been recorded. One example is the so-called Einstein-Podolsky-Rosen paradox, initially invented among others by Albert Einstein to prove that quantum mechanics is incorrect, or at least incomplete. The paradox goes like this: when two particles of opposite "spin" fly apart, changing the spin of one would simultaneously change the spin of the other – even when they are at opposite ends of the world (Keutzer 1984, 85). This means, they can either communicate at speed faster than light (considered impossible by Einstein and relativity-theory) or they are not "things," and not separate (impossible by common-sense). But the impossible seems to be proven, at the latest in the Innsbruck experiment 1998 and the Boulder-experiment 2001, while Bell´s theorem has given the mathematical foundation (Cf. Drobisch 2009, 45-47). Summing up earlier experiments and their implications, Bernard d´Espagnat (1979) of the university of Paris concluded, "the violation of separability seems to imply that in some sense all these objects constitute an indivisible whole" (cited after Keutzer 1984, 86). The psychologist Keutzer goes on in the same line, stating that accepting non-locality means embracing the temporal paradoxes of an instantaneously connected world in which nothing really can be separated from anything else (Keutzer 1984, 86). "Bell´s proof of a non-local ultimate reality is thus the contemporary echo from mathematics of the ancient mystical claim "we are all one"" (Ibid.).

Jung, who considered his research concerning synchronicity to run parallel to the developments in quantum physics, made the same conclusions as Keutzer and d´Espagnat concerning ESP and other synchronistic phenomena. Since a causal explanation for above reasons seems impossible, Jung concludes that the ESP phenomena must constitute a psychically induced relativization of time and space - a concourse or coincidence in time and space; in other words a sort of *synchronicity* (Jung 1990, 24). In the spatial experiment setting is space, and in the temporal setting is time approximately reduced to zero – or coinciding in a point – as earlier described characteristic for the magic consciousness. This means by implication that the experiments suggest that time and space stand in a relationship with mental conditions - or that time and space as such even do not exist, but first are "set" through the consciousness. As outlined earlier, space and time as "solid" concepts are indeed late achievements in consciousness development that depends on measurement, characteristic for the mental stage – while for instance the archaic and magic consciousness structure as was previously argued lives in a pre-temporal and pre-spatial condition. Jung notes as well in this line that space and time are dubious categories among the "primitives," and as hypostazised terms only come to existence through the discriminating activity of the consciousness, where they constitute the necessary coordinates for the account of moving bodies (Ibid.). Since I earlier have placed consciousness as equal to spirit, it can be argued that *space and time primarily are of spiritual origin* – albeit it appears differently for the waking consciousness. This, then, is also in agreement with Dietrich´s outline of the yoga-philosophy, when he associates space-time awareness to *Vishudda*, the transpersonal sphere beyond the mental layer (Dietrich, 2015; 88). If space and time, however, are products of *consciousness* – as opposed to the material aspect of *energy*, and the human psyche is composed of both – then the relativization of both by the human psyche is at least not impossible. At this point I would like to remind the reader that about the formless and immediate awareness of the Witness it was said that she sees not the world, because she is the world, and apprehends it subjectively as "self-sense" or self-felt and not as outer object (Cf. Dietrich 2011, 382). This is the case when the mind does not observe outer objects but *itself*, which exactly is what happens in the case of ESP. In Rhine´s experiments the test subject gives the answer not through seeing the physical cards, but through pure imagination, that is, a conscious idea in the mind. Images (and more generally ideas) that rise spontaneously to consciousness are themselves manifestations of the unconsciousness. The unconscious itself consists in the earlier outlined archaic, magic and mythic structures – and in some sense also in the integral, global and non-dual structures. Interesting in this observation is that the ESP phenomena on the one hand is a true child of the magic consciousness in its pre-temporal and pre-spatial point-like unity, dependent on the emotional involvement of the test-subject – and on the other hand fits the description of the global Witness awareness, in its knowing of the world through self-awareness. This observation in itself underpins my earlier suggestion concerning the close relationship between the magic and the global layer.

3.1.2. Synchronicity and Correspondence

The psychologist Kirby Surprise points out that Rhine´s experiments would suggest the overall ability to influence the outside world synchronistically is a few percentages (Surprise 2012, 31-32). In other words, if I gamble and roll dices with the intent to produce sixes, I heighten the chance to actually produce sixes by a few percentages – as pointed out earlier; some are better in this regard than others. These numbers have of course to be taken with caution and seen in context of the recorded circumstances, as for instance the reduced and clinical setting. For instance, if I want to influence my chances in winning the lottery, the numbers might be different. Another clinical setting where effects lacking a causal explanation are recorded is in the famous placebo effect, which is measured to have up to a 35 percent chance of giving therapeutic effect (Beecher 1955, 1602). Here too, positive expectation and faith seem to be the decisive factors – in other words the emotional quality of the inner state of the patient. However, in the case of the placebo effect, which regards the own body, causal explanations are likely, as the emotional quality has measurable influence on – or rather goes hand in hand with - the body chemistry, and therefore does not count as synchronicity.

While the effect of synchronistic intervention thus arguably is small, it might be just enough to tip the scales. One question in regards to synchronicity is thus how far inner-psychic states synchronistically influence outer states and circumstances. In order to demonstrate that this is a peace-scientifically relevant question, I need only refer to the story of the Taoist Rainmaker. This story, which by now has the status of a legend in transpersonal and humanistic orientated circles, is an actually occurred event witnessed by Richard Wilhelm and told by him to Jung. Dietrich uses it as a paradigmatic (and probably mostly allegorical) example of transrational peace-work (Dietrich 2011, 29-30). However, this story is not only an impressive example of what transrational peace-work is all about, but also an impressive example of what synchronicity is all about. Hence follows the slightly lengthy story of the rainmaker of Kiaochau as told by Jung:

> There was great drought. For months there had not been a drop of rain and the situation became catastrophic. The Catholics made processions, the Protestants made prayers and the Chinese burned joss stick, and shot off guns to frighten away the demons of the drought, but with no result. Finally the Chinese said, "We will fetch the rainmaker." And from another province a dried-up old man appeared. The only thing he had asked for was a quiet little house somewhere, and there he locked himself in for three days. On the fourth day the clouds gathered and there was a great snow storm at the time of the year when no snow was expected, an unusual amount, and the town was so full of rumors about the wonderful rainmaker that Richard Wihelm went to ask the man how he did it. In true European fashion he said, "they call you the rainmaker, will you tell me how you made the snow?" And the little Chinese man said, "I did not make the snow, I am not responsible. " "But what have you done these three days?" "Oh, I can explain that. I come from another country where things are in order. Here they are out of order, they are not as they should be by the ordinance of heaven. Therefore the whole country is not in Tao, and I also am not in the natural order of things because I am in a disordered country. So I had to wait three days until I was back in Tao and then naturally the rain came (Jung 1979, 419-420).

What among other things can be seen in this example is a prime case of synchronicity. First the outer circumstances are stated to reflect into the inner circumstances of the old man, which causally can be explained by stating that a drought, and the depressed and desperate state of the people would obviously affect the old rainmaker's mood and psychic state. The clear synchronicity sets in when "naturally the rain came" once the old man had regained his inner balance. Peace-work when at its best. The question of synchronicity is here implicated in the question - *why would outer circumstances follow – or rather coincide – with inner psychic states?* The connected and likewise intricate and relevant question is: how can a single person become the center of coincidences affecting a whole country? While these are rather complicated matters, there is hope and comfort for the practical aspect of the individual peace work: simply being at peace can save a whole country! Especially interesting in this example is again the relation between the global and the personal; beginning with a global perspective when the old man first states that he comes from a country, which is in order, for which reason he consequently is in order himself. The next step is also comprehensible, when he comes to a country in distress and finds himself feeling out of order as well. The crux of the matter is the next step – how do outer states in the environment follow, or coincide with, the inner-psychic state of the old rainmaker, without any physical intervention?

3.1.2.1. The Magic Mirror

The experience that inner-psychic states influence outer events beyond space and time – or rather, the practice to influence outer events by manipulating inner-psychic states, goes back at least to the neolithic age, and has roots in the magic consciousness. In the caves of Les Trois Freres, France, are some of the world's oldest cave paintings. One of the images is a shaman wearing a stag mask, which most likely is a depiction of a magical rite. The tribe hoped the shaman could, by his imitation of the prey, make the stag appear during the hunt (Surprise 2012, 32). Another example is the earlier described hunting-scene by Leo Frobius. Contemporary variations are for instance made public in Rhonda Byrne´s (2006) popular book "The Secret," and to some extent also all forms of autogenic training – where the former explicitly hopes for synchronistic effects, which are believed to rest on a universal 'law of attraction,' the latter aiming more for causal lines of effect. Albeit I would argue that some of its success rests on the accompanying synchronistic occurrences. At the core of all such magic beliefs there often eventually and intuitively develops a guiding principle of correspondence between microcosm and macrocosm, the human and the world/universe, where the two are seen as *dynamic* mirror images of each other. This means, when one moves, the other moves as well. As a rough and simplified guiding frame, I could state that in magic (egocentric) frames of reference the world is seen as mirror-image of the human – while in mythic frames of reference the human is eventually seen as mirror-image of the world. The distinction is important for the practice, because it never makes sense to try to alter the mirror image. Consequently, the magic logic seeks to alter the world/mirror by manipulating the self, while mythic logic prays to and manipulates the world in order to alter the mirror/self. For completion, it might be added that mental logic, neither dwelling in magic unity or mythic polarity but in duality between self and world, manipulates both self and world, without seeing the synchronistic connection between self and world – and in its ego-consciousness mostly dwells on the own physical mirror-image, and puts mirrors in front of other mammals in order to see if they as well are capable of this particular form of self-referentiality. In both magic and mythic variations of the correspondence principle it is valid to learn about the self by looking at the world and vice versa – which is why in both variations ESP, prophecy, visions, etc., are possible (learning about the world through the self), as well as all forms of divination (learning about the self through the world).

In how far these synchronistic effects are of transpersonal character and/or (rather) belong to a pre-personal magic and mythic "time" and consciousness – in how far we are dealing with the inner workings of the All-One – and how this affects peace-work - will in the following be investigated in depth by discussing Jung's psychology of the archetypes, which is closely related to his concept of synchronicity.

3.2. Jungian Psychology

Carl Gustav Jung, the founder of analytical psychology, dissident student of Sigmund Freud, and author of more than 50 books, was born in 1875 in Kesswil, Switzerland. He grew up as an introverted and fragile only child, tending to daydreams and fantasies, but eventually developed into a robust, hard-drinking and extroverted student of medicine (Peat 1989, 18). When Jung met the older and well-established Sigmund Freud in 1907, Jung had with his word association test and his complex theory already accomplished significant contributions to the field of psychology. The meeting and discussion of the two men proved to be exceedingly fruitful. For Jung it was "*ein 'religiöser' Zusammenstoß mit unleugbar erotischen Obertönen,*" while Freud wrote: "*Ich hätte mir niemand besseren als Dich wünschen können, um meine Arbeit fortzusetzen und zu vervollständigen*" (Cited after Peat 1989, 18). Jung's advancement within the Vienna Organization was comet-like; 1908 he organizes the first international Congress in Salzburg and became elected President of the International Psychoanalytical Association. Nevertheless, in their respective approaches to the unconscious, Freud and Jung diverged greatly. While Freud came from a rational, scientific tradition, and was convinced that the unconscious consisted of instincts and suppressions, over which the thin layer of civilization was placed, Jung were more interested in spirituality, fantasy, and the strange paintings of his patients; convinced that the unconsciousness was a hidden, creative dimension, not solely ruled by the libido (Ibid. 19).

Already in 1909, while still close friends, the first strong clash in their relationship occurred. One day Freud blamed Jung for his interest in spiritualism, warning him against being "overrun by the black wave of occult filth." In this moment Jung felt a burning hot sensation in his diaphragm, and in the same moment both of them heard a loud crack from the bookshelf. Jung commented that this would be an instance of "catalytically exteriorization," to which Freud replied "utter nonsense." Jung predicted that another instance would happen immediately. And so it was; another loud crack sounded, which terrified Freud considerably (Ibid.). This "catalytically exteriorization," I would also label synchronistic event (SE), and the fact that Jung, already at that time, had an at least terminological conceptualization of such phenomena demonstrates that he not only was aware of and consciously experiencing such phenomena, but also considered the external, material manifestation of psychic events a reality - although more than forty years were to pass before his actual treatise on synchronicity was written.

A couple of years after the above described incident, Jung continued his research in a completely different direction than prescribed by Freud, while the final break in their relationship occurred in 1912 (Ibid.). From that time on Jung began to freely develop his psychology.

3.2.1. The Unconscious

If the person had classically been considered to consist of soul, spirit and body, Freud took this triadic structure of the person and revolutionized it; formulating the person to consist in an above superego, which corresponds to superimposed societal values and norms, the below id, which is led by drives, and the consciously judging and acting ego in the middle, mediating between the two of them (Dietrich 2008, 355). Jung kept this threefold structure, but being more interested in the unconscious, he relocated his focus and formulated the psychological person to consist of (1) ego-consciousness, (2) the personal unconscious, and (3) the collective unconscious.

Ego-consciousness does in Jungian terminology basically denote the sum-total of everything that is known to the person and corresponds thus to what I earlier simply have termed consciousness. Jung supposed the ego to be placed at the center of the field of consciousness, as the necessary subjective factor without which consciousness itself would not exist (Aziz 1990, 19). As such, Jung seems to take the ego for granted, while, as argued earlier, the awareness of the ego not is naturally given, and Jung also states that ego-consciousness is a relatively late evolutionary acquisition (Jung 1964, 23). The personal unconscious he describes as residing at the periphery of consciousness, and contains all those contents that are forgotten, or repressed biographical experiences, as well as subliminally received information (Jacobi 1978, 31). In contrast to the personal unconscious, whose contents are acquired, the contents of the collective unconscious are indigenous to the psyche (Ibid. 32). These contents are imagined to lie in even further peripheries, consisting of the drives and the archetypes (Ibid. 30). The word collective referred to 'the beginning,' in other words to the early Jung´s understanding that that this part of the unconscious is evolutionary inherited, and thus common to all humans, as is a nose or a beating heart. A common misunderstanding used to be to imagine the collective as field-phenomena, which is shared by all people. Ironically, while fighting this misunderstanding most of his life, in the end, and due to the synchronicity-hypothesis, Jung himself describes the collective unconscious as a sort of atmosphere, containing all the individual (un)consciousnesses (Adler and Jaffé 1975, 433). Meanwhile, and in both understandings does the collective unconscious imply, that humans would not be born as blank sheets and solely accumulate unconscious content during their lifetime, as Freud were assuming, but are already filled with content – that is, psychologically speaking. Roughly put, Jung´s collective unconscious thus corresponds to the earlier outlined three first chakra, and the three last chakra, while the fourth chakra, anahata, is the necessary meeting point that enables individual consciousness. Hence, in transrational psychology there exists both a lower collective unconsciousness and a higher collective 'super'-consciousness, which, however, is a differentiation not made by Jung.

Crucial for Jung´s psychology is the relationship between the conscious and the unconscious, which is described as compensatory. In the following I will relate how Jung came to recognize the latter via dream-analysis, in order to better understand the compensatory activity of the unconscious, the archetypes, and their symbolical implications.

3.2.1.1. Archetypes and Symbolism

It was among others Freud´s genius, which recognized that neurotic symptoms as hysteria, certain types of pain, and abnormal behavior are symbolically meaningful. For instance, a person who is confronted with an intolerable situation may develop a spasm whenever he tries to swallow: corresponding to the proverb "He can´t swallow it." Another confronted with similar circum-stances may develop a paralysis of the legs; "She can´t go on anymore." "They are one way in which the unconscious mind expresses itself, just as it may in dreams; and they are equally symbolic" (Jung 1964, 26).

One major quarrel and divergence between Jung´s understanding, and Freud´s psychology, arose exactly out of the role they attached to dreams and their interpretation. Both agreed that dreams originated in the unconscious. Freud, who as earlier indicated believed the unconsciousness to be of solely personal character, and consisting of drives and their suppressions, consequently considered libidinous wish fulfillment, and unconscious repressions of the libido as the sole causes of dream symbolism and neurotic behavior. In other words, Freud reduced the unconscious psyche to the second chakra. He made the observation, that if the dreamer is encouraged to talk about her dream images, and the thoughts and associations they prompt in her mind, she will give herself away and reveal the unconscious background for her ailments, in both what she says and in what she deliberately omits (Jung 1964, 27). While Freud attached special importance to dreams as the point of departure for those "free associations," Jung discovered that in fact any topic, a casual conversation for instance, can be used as departure for "free associations," and still inevitably lead to the habitual complexes (this are the tender spots of the psyche, which react quickly to external stimulus or disturbance) (Ibid.). Thus, Jung considered this technique a waste of the rich dream images of his patients, and felt that he should treat the dream images in their own right and as genuine messages from the unconsciousness, potentially symbolizing other significant things than conflicts between the sexual drive and social necessities.

> A man may dream of inserting a key in a lock, of wielding a heavy stick, or of breaking down a door with a battering ram. Each of these can be regarded as a sexual allegory. But the fact that his unconscious for its own purposes has chosen one of the specific images – it may be the key, the stick, or the battering ram – is also of major significance. The real task is to understand why the key has been preferred to the stick, or the stick to the ram. And sometimes this might even lead one to discover that it is not the sexual act at all that is represented, but some quite different psychological point (Jung 1964, 27).

It is here that Jung differentiates the mythic structure from Freud´s sole reduction to the magic structure, when Jung acknowledges that each of these hypothetical dream-pictures can be regarded as sexual allegory (second chakra/magic), but simultaneously also may represented as other psychological points (third chakra/mythic). The thus freed study of his patients' dream images in their own rights, and the simultaneous comparative study of symbols and symbolism in history, along with religions and mythologies from all times and all over the world enabled Jung to make several highly valuable insights. Due to his knowledge of mythological symbols and images, he saw that his patients' dream images in many cases already existed as symbols in ancient mythologies or religions – often completely foreign to the dreamer[34]. Jung relates for instance one case, where a professor who had had a sudden vision and thought he was insane, came to see him. Jung simply took a 400-year old book from the shelf and showed him an old woodcut depicting his very vision, saying "There´s no reason for you to believe that you are insane. They knew about your vision 400 years ago." whereupon the professor sat down entirely deflated, but once more normal (Jung 1964, 69). It were the accumulation of cases like this and similar ones, which led Jung to deduce the existence of a collective unconscious, able to produce exactly the same pictures, themes and symbols all over the world in vastly different time-periods. Since these collective symbols, which came up in those dreams Jung were analyzing, used to belong in religious and spiritual traditions (in former times basically everything did), Jung concluded that religions and mythologies are both (collective) dream pictures and visions from

[34] Freud has to be credited for first observing and commenting on those elements in a dream that are not individual and that cannot be derived from the dreamer's personal experience. He called them "archaic remnants" and considered them basically meaningless (Ibid). Jung has to be credited for actually making sense of those "archaic remnants".

former times, and also have their origin in the collective unconscious. This underlines and corresponds to Gebser's findings concerning the mythic structure and strongly suggests that Jung here is differentiating the mythic structure from Freud's sole reduction to the magic structure. Taken for what they were, and not just reduced to sexual or other instinctual patterns, these symbols were often expressing highly sophisticated moral and philosophical concepts, which for Jung proved that there were other, meaningful and intelligent forces at work in the unconscious, more precisely the collective unconscious, besides the drives and instincts – which perfectly corresponds to the mythic structure being connected to intelligence. Those other factors at work in the unconscious besides the drives, which Jung assumed to produce intelligent dream-pictures and symbolic behavior, he called the archetypes – and arguably Jung did indeed have tendencies to reduce the whole unconscious to the archetypes as expressed in the mythic structure.

One point to highlight is that, just as with the battering ram, the key and the stick, the same topic or motif can be symbolized in a great variety. This is important for Jung's understanding of the archetypes, because the Jungian archetypes are not synonymous or equal with Plato's *Ideas* or *Forms* (also Jung himself was fond of thinking so) or a definite mythological image, which is a common misunderstanding. Jung understood the archetypes as creative *tendencies* to form representations of a motif – representations that can vary great in detail without losing its basic pattern (Jung 1964, 67). The archetype of the great Mother is thus not an ideal form of the great Mother, but a potential tendency, which can become represented in the form of for instance Demeter, Ishtar, Astarte, Shakti, Lakshmi, the ocean or a forest – while, as already indicated, not only the specific form the archetype manifests itself in is significant, but also the circumstance that someone from whose cultural background one would assume would dream of Maria, the mother of Christ, actually might dream of the black Kali with blood-dripping skulls around her neck, without ever having encountered this image in personal life. The picture of Kali would then highlight a different aspect of the great Mother archetype than Maria would, also individual interpretations are more complex than this, and do not follow any prescript in Jungian analysis. Important at this point is to note that the archetype-as-such is something quite different than the archetypal image it produces.

The early Jung described the archetypes as formal factors that pattern unconscious processes; they are "patterns of behaviour" (sic) (Jung 1990, 25). At the same time they are archetypes not void of energy, but have a specific charge, which means they unfold numinous effects, which express themselves as emotions (or affects). These emotions (as do emotions generally) cause a partial lowering of the conscious level, a *partielles abaissement du niveau mental,* through heightening a specific content to above-normal clarity, which simultaneously withdraws correspondingly much energy from other possible conscious content, and leaves this other possibilities obscured respectively unconscious[35] (Ibid.). Due to this clouded awareness brought about by the emotion, a lowered sense of orientation accrues for the time being, which again allows more unconscious material to break into the empty room. Thus, Jung explains, it is a common experience that in emotional states unexpected and otherwise suppressed - respectively unconscious - material breaks through and comes to utterance (Ibid.). These utterances are often of inferior or primitive nature and do thus reveal their origin in the archetypes, and when this process occurs, Jungians say an archetype is constellated (Ibid.). The constellation of an archetype with the accompanying emotional charge, in case it 'takes over' the respective person, consequently correspond to a temporary descend to lower chakra levels by simultaneously abandoning higher structures. In the following paragraph I will outline Jung´s thoughts on the depths of the archetypes.

3.2.1.2. The Archetype as Psychoid Factor

In his 1924 essay "Instinct and the Unconscious" Jung describes the unconscious as consisting of the discontinuous, yet functionally complementary pair of instincts and archetypes.

> Instincts are typical modes of action, and wherever we meet with uniform and regularly recurring modes of action and reaction we are dealing with instinct... Archetypes are typical modes of apprehension, and wherever we meet with uniform and regularly recurring modes of apprehension we are dealing with an archetype (Jung 1969b, 137-138).

In illustrating how the instinct and the archetype complement each other, he gives the example of the yucca moth, which only once in its life, and on the sole evening where the yucca plant opens, must shape the pollen of one flower into a pellet and insert it into the pistil of a second flower. It is as if the yucca moth "must carry within it an image, as it were, of the situation that "trigger´s off" its instinct. This image enables it to "recognize" the yucca flower and it´s structure" (Ibid.).

As the attentive reader notices, Jung, in the citation above states that archetypes are patterns of behavior - and not pattern of apprehension as just quoted. This implied theoretical shift, where Jung fused the archetype with the instincts, occurred in 1946 as outlined in his paper "On the Nature of the

[35] Which probably is why the proverb correctly states: Love makes one blind.

Psyche," where he now views these two factors, archetype and instinct, as part of a continuum.

> Archetype and instinct are the most polar opposites imaginable, as can easily be seen when one compares a man who is ruled by his instinctual drives with one who is seized by the spirit. But, just as between all opposites there obtains so close a bond that no position can be established or even thought of without its corresponding negation, so in this case also "les extremes se touchent" (Jung 1969, 206).

He goes on drawing attention to the close relationship that emerges in religious phenomenology between what are supposed to be the deadly enemies of physical and spiritual passion. In reality, Jung suggests, these enemies are indeed "brothers-in-arms, for which reason it often needs the merest touch to convert the one into the other" (Ibid. 212). Basically, what Jung now does, is to ground this complementary pair of archetype and instinct in an oneness. What he formerly called archetype he now refers to as spirit, that is, the innate pattern of meaning, while instinct remains the innate pattern of action. Consequently, the archetype-as-such is not a subsequent synthesis of two pre-existing factors, but an antecedent oneness in an yet undifferentiated state – which eventually (or potentially) differentiates into the complementary pair of spirit and instinct. The archetypal image and the instinct thus emerge from the same undifferentiated root, which Jung called the *psychoid,* but retain their quality as opposites engaged in a more or less constant tension with each other. From this tension the energy of the psyche is generated, and given a peculiar character (Progoff 1973, 81). This unification of spirit and instinct is a point of major relevance, since Jung here in his own terms describes the coincidence of Alpha and Omega – the coincidence of the telluric and the cosmic epicenter. The conclusion is that Jung asserts a unitary aspect of being, the *Unus Mundus,* as metaphysical background for the synchronicity between psyche and matter. This yet undifferentiated archetype-as-such, which lies at the ground of existence, becomes thus another term for the Epicenter, Being-as-such, the Alpha and Omega of consciousness, the place where observer and observed are one, something Jung in reference to alchemists termed the "Unus Mundus" - the one-world - or in other words, the All-One.

Transferred to the earlier outlined model, this looks as depicted in the following figure, where the two arrows stand for the complementary movements and differentiation of instinct and spirit respectively, grounded in the same undifferentiated oneness, which in terms of consciousness meet at the mental ego-level. Obviously this does not mean that the pre-personal side solely consist of instinct and the trans-personal solely of spirit – but as the above outline remarks, instinct and spirit do at all times interpenetrate each other, and in the end constitute two aspects of the same thing. The only thing that changes is the human awareness or consciousness - moving as earlier described clockwise –and whether consciousness is blind and ruled by instinct - or whether instinct has become "enlightened" and ruled by consciousness.

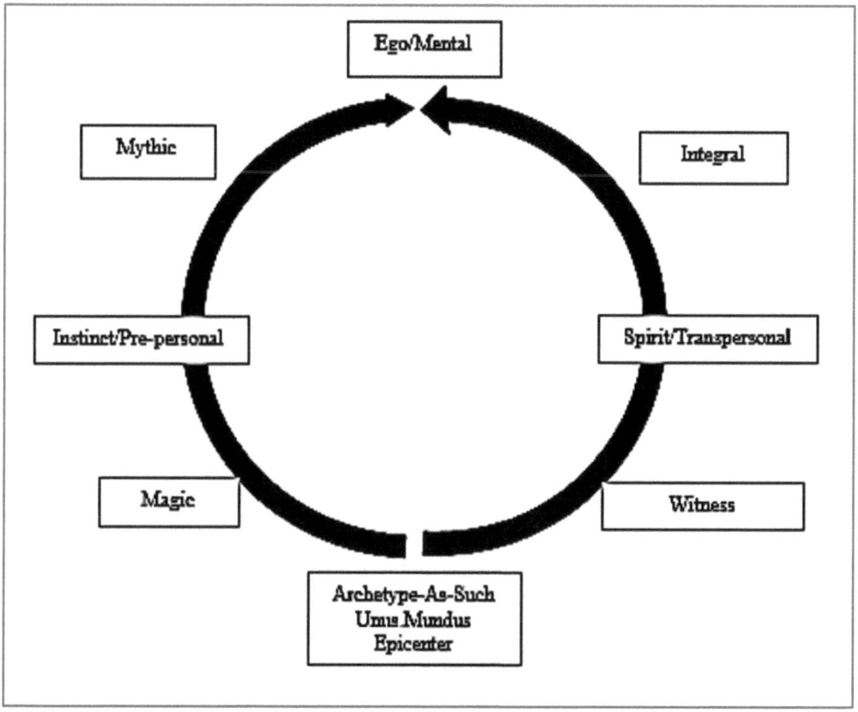

Figure 2: The differentiation of the archetype-as-such in relation to the different layers.

Important for Jung´s recognition of the archetype as a *psychoid* factor, that is, a psychophysical factor, which in Jung´s understanding ultimately means a continuum between and basic oneness of psyche and matter, were as mentioned his experiences with synchronicity.

> Since psyche and matter are contained in one and the same world, and moreover are in continuous contact with one another and ultimately rest on irrepresentable, transcendental factors, it is not only possible but fairly probable, even, that psyche and matter are two different aspects of one and the same thing. The synchronicity phenomena point, it seems to me, in this direction, for they show that the nonpsychic can behave like the psychic and vice versa, without there being any causal connection between them (Jung 1969, 215)

Evidently, Jung does not reduce psyche to physiological processes, but in a pantheistic manner unite both in one and the same reality. Ira Progoff (1973), whose paper on synchronicity and Jung´s perspective was revised by Jung himself, points out that the *psychoid* level of development corresponds in the microcosm to the primal chaos of the universe/macrocosm, just as the individualized and microcosmic archetype of the Self, the God-image, is a reflection of the macrocosmic universe (Progoff 1973, 79-80).

3.2.1.3. Synchronicities as Creative Acts in Time

As already pointed out, Jung understands synchronistic events (SE´s) as acausally connected phenomena, with *meaning* as its *tertium comparationis* (Jung 1990, 63). The consequences are clear: if the connection is acausal, and one and the same meaning manifests in the individual as well as the surrounding, then meaning itself, or at least some meaningfulness, is natural and prior to the individual and social construction of meaning. This contradicts (post) modern academic common sense, which assumes that human beings are the solely ones constructing and attributing meaning to the world. The alternative is just as horrific to the academic common sense, since, as Jung points out, we then would have to assume some *magic* causality to influence the events (Ibid., 64). As Jung further notes, tradition does not help much in the choice between transcendental meaning and magic causality, since many cultures up to this day claim magic causality to be at the root of synchronicities, while continental philosophy since antiquity and up until the 18th century has assumed mystical *correspondentia* in natural phenomena; that is, analogous pattern or meaning-connections (Ibid.). Having been engaged most of his professional life with searching and finding meaning in the products of the unconsciousness; it seems natural for Jung to choose the transcendental meaning, patterned by his hypothetical archetypes. Jung further preferred the latter explanation, since he believed that the notion of some form of magic causality would interfere with the common notion of causality (Ibid.). Jung´s strategy to safeguard his theories always consisted in confining his subject to the psyche, away from the reach of other sciences. As such, his notion of *acausality* perform the double task of placing the subject of synchronicity outside the reach, and without interfering in the established common sense worldview – besides also satisfying Jung´s almost obsessive engagement with opposites. If there exist causality, there must also exist acausality. The blueprint for the notion of acausality Jung found in Leibnitz's notion of the pre-established harmony, where mind and matter are thought not to be in contact with one another, but synchronized into a perfect meaningful parallelism, which itself was an answer and attempt to balance the earlier by Descartes' formulated mind-matter duality- and as such, a rather doubtful notion. However, this finally lead Jung to re-formulate what he considered the triad of the classical physical worldview, namely time, space and causality into the quaternio of space, time, causality and synchronicity (Ibid. 91):

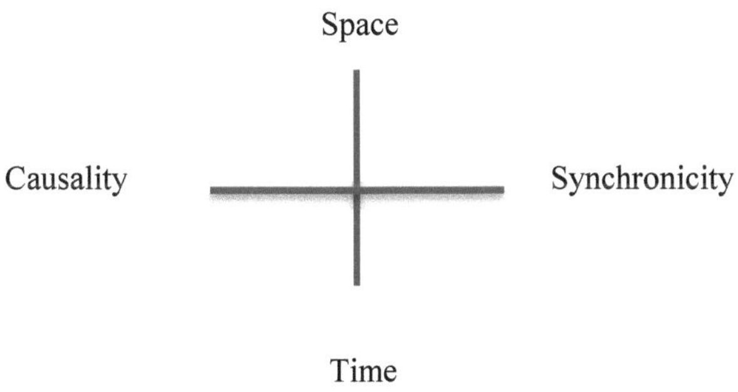

Figure 3: the quaternio of space, time, causality and synchronicity after Jung (1990, 91).

Representative for Jung´s reasoning is the circumstance, that he sees it as a great advantage of this tetradic formulation, that it repeats and solves a problem which has been running like a red thread for a millennia and a half through the speculations of the alchemistic philosophy; namely the so-called *axiom of Maria*: *ek tú tritú to he tetarton* (from the third follows the one as fourth) (Ibid.). Gerardus Dorneus, an alchemist of the 16th century, recognized the dilemma between the three and the four, the decision between the Christian trinity and the heathen *serpens quadricornutus* (the four-horned snake), with the four deriving from the two, which symbolizes matter, the feminine and the devil[36] (cited after Jung 1990, 92). This symbolical shift from the four to the three Jung noticed on several front lines, as for instance when the correspondence-doctrine of Robert Fludd had to give way for the three-principal-doctrine of Johannes Kepler, on which there followed a scientific era ruled by time, space and causality. Here, Jung sees the discontinuities of quantum physics breaking with this classical physical worldview, and hopes the time ripe to re-introduce the quaternio (Ibid.) – analogous to the trans-rational shift described by Wolfgang Dietrich, who sees the post-moderns figuratively killing the god Apollo, symbolically standing for the triadic one truth, and re-vitalizing Dionysus, the symbolically energetic, devil and feminine aspect of life (Dietrich 2008, 317).

[36] This dilemma is also the topic of another of Jung´s more famous SE´s, where he while walking along the shore of a lake, pondering the conflict between the Christian and the alchemical worldview, found a snake which had died in the attempt to swallow a fish. The serpent being a symbol of the alchemists and the fish the symbol of Christ, Jung found this incident confirming his conviction that these two philosophies indeed are incommensurable.

In collaboration with his physician friend Wolfgang Pauli, Jung incorporated the newer findings of physics into his quaternio, which then looks as follows (Jung, 1990, 93):

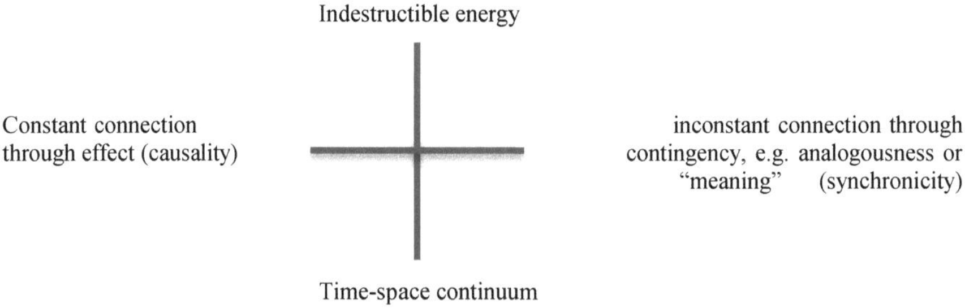

Figure 4: The extended quaternio after Jung (1990, 93).

Relevant for me in this model, which itself figuratively unites relativity theory with the discontinuities of quantum mechanics, is the description of synchronicity, or synchronistic connections, as contingent in relation to causal determination. This means they are 'carried' or attached to the causal chains, but not determined or governed by those. As such, Jung imagines synchronicity as special cases of a general contingency, a lawlessness or randomness, which completely regularly is carried through time. What Jung has in mind is the modality of creation, of the very beginning – the random premise on which the law is built – a just-so-ness – Gebser′s ever present origin. This is a logic consequence, if he wants to keep synchronicities as acausally connected phenomena. Having previously connected synchronistic events to the constellation of archetypes, the latter are consequently now counted to the contingent phenomena, and as such gain a status or modus which functionally is a world constitutive factor (Ibid.), a not further reducible just-so-ness or un-caused arrangement. However, differentiating between contingent arrangements of whole numbers and discontinuities of physics that can be found at all times, synchronicities, which according to Jung cannot be found at all times, do then constitute *creative acts in time* (Ibid. 95).

In the same line, warning against understanding the archetype to *cause* the SE, Jung remains stuck for an answer on how the creative archetype brings about the meaningful pattern. In an attempt to address the problem, Ira Progoff gets closer but remains circumventing the issue, when writing:

> The principle at work is apparently an interior one, although something in its nature enables it to extend across time and space. It does not directly change events or conditions in themselves, but it brings about a reordering of the pattern of things within which specific situations and conditions are contained. Context and meanings thus change imperceptibly. Since a factor of

> change is involved, we may say that there is a "power" at work, and that this should be characterized as a form of energy. We may suppose further that this energy would be capable of causal analysis if it were only not so subtle and intangible as to prevent us from laying our hands on it and dissecting it. On closer look, however, we see that it would not be correct for us to speak of this "power" as energy, for we would then be postulating it as a definite factor, as an entity that is itself involved in the situation. When a pattern is set up in time by the activation of an archetype, however, the crucial factor does not seem to be an external agency of any kind but rather an ordering principle that is inherent in the fact that a pattern is being formed. What holds the pattern together, then, is not a vector of energy but an interior cohesion, some principle of interior binding that operates within and across the prevailing pattern, maintaining the pattern as a whole in terms of the interior correspondence of its constituent parts (Progoff 1973, 86-87).

What Progoff here tries to describe I believe is commonly called spirit and the 'glue,' that interior binding is *meaning* itself, or Tao, which is this famous Chinese concept Richard Wilhelm translated exactly to *meaning*.

3.2.2. Archetypes and Healing

The archetypes are here of special interest, because Jung associated synchronistic events with the constellation of archetypes. The earlier described process of how the conscious level is lowered through emotional states is thus also applicable to describe the dynamics found in for instance shamanistic rituals and mediumistic trance. Here the shaman sets him/herself in an emotionally charged state, typically through drumming, dancing, and singing, while mediums set themselves in equally emotional and hypnotic states through hypnotic techniques like focusing on candle-light and other conventional triggers[37]. What Jung calls the accruing lowering of the consciousness level is in my terminology thus describable as a decent to, or rather "opening up" for direct experience of lower chakra consciousness – especially the magic level with its characteristic of emotional point like unity. In this state, as pointed out earlier, synchronistic events seem to underline phenomena operating outside of (and in the context of consciousness I should say prior to) time and space manifesting themselves. Congruent with these remarks is that Dietrich associates traditional and shamanistic *healing* with the second chakra, the intra-personal layer of sexuality and the inter-personal layer of the family (Dietrich 2011, 364). While Dietrich masterfully explains the relationship between sexuality and family, and how these layers influences all levels of the persona and the wider organization – and

[37] Interestingly Werner J. Meinhold argues that the archaic state (prenatal to 2 years old) corresponds to a deep hypnosis, magic consciousness corresponds to deep to middle deep hypnosis, the mythic state to light hypnosis and the mental structure (12 – 14 years onwards) to overtly awake consciousness with partial hypnotic states (Meinhold 1997, 129-131).

how modern psychology exactly sets in on the second chakra level – it is only here with the further association to magic consciousness, emotional point like unity and synchronistic phenomena, that the connections to - and processes of - traditional shamanistic healing become more obvious and understandable in this context. In the frame of this outline I have thus reason to assume that traditional healer typically work with their emotional self, in other frameworks conceptualized as the astral-body, on and with the emotional self of the patient. In how far emotions can influence healing has already been indicated with the placebo effect. The commonly missed point however is the non-local quality of emotions to work beyond (or prior to) space and time, and thus manifest symbolical correspondences. To recapitulate: commonly accepted is that emotional states such as personal complexes and neurosis can express themselves symbolically in and on the person (in form of symbolically corresponding dreams, phantasies, spasms, etc.). The synchronicity-concept simply adds the empirical observation that the same emotions also manifest in symbolical correspondences outside of the person. Ritual healing thus applies in logical consequence the same dynamic in reverse, when symbolically corresponding medicine or actions intend to influence the emotional state – and in further consequence the whole person. The connection between ideas, dreams and phantasies on the one hand, and emotions on the other, is sufficiently established[38]. Worth mentioning again, however, is the earlier established description of magic consciousness as equal to dream-states. This might account for the shamanic descriptions of 'soul-journeys' and 'spirit-travels,' as symbolically corresponding cognitive experience to the emotional states in the ritual – where the shaman enters deeply and lucidly into the magic dream-state. That these dream states and the emotional bond between the shaman and the patient is inter-subjectively quite real, and at times very dramatic, and does not constitute mere personal phantasies and disconnected random events, where the only healing effect is the placebo-effect, is suggested by events as the following related by Mircea Eliade;

> A shaman was trying to bring back the soul of a woman who had died suddenly, when he fell dead himself from a terrible wound in his stomach. A second shaman entered the scene and revived the woman, whereupon she related that she had seen the first shaman´s spirit crossing a lake in the form of a walrus (his primal form?), and that someone had hit him with a weapon, the effect of the blow being visible on the corpse (Eliade 1964, 383).

[38] Neuroscientific research has for instance demonstrated that electrical stimulation of a certain brain area can cause the test-subject to laugh, while the "story" of what was funny every time changed and clearly followed after the stimulation – while normally the "story" triggers a stimulation of the specific brain area. The relationship between ideas, emotions and neurobiological processes is thus a two-way street (Cf. Fried et al.: "Electric current stimulates laughter" in *Nature* **391**, 650 (12 February 1998)).

While this example involve concepts (for instance the personal soul), and dynamics (for instance where this soul goes after death), which to analyze and account for go beyond the scope of this paper, it also involves and exemplifies those general dynamics which I try to outline, especially the closeness of shaman and patient in the ritual act. The by the shaman established emotional identification goes so far that the woman even can recognize the shaman in their now shared dream-state. The shaman who now shares dream and destiny with the woman, but is unable to restore the woman and drag her with him back to waking life, inevitably shares her fate of dropping dead, while his death in the magic consciousness symbolically (or rather synchronistically) manifests as a wound in his stomach.

The bond between shaman and patient I assume to be one akin to lucid emotional identification. Identification between persons is normally described as unconscious and marked by transference and counter-transference phenomena. In agreement with this assumption, and with respect to SE´s within which both healer and patient are contained, or in a modern psychological setting analyst and analysand, Jung suggests that SE´s do seem to increase in proportion to the degree of unconscious identification between the analyst and analysand (Jung 1989, 137). Since people seeing SE´s often are 'charged' of falling victim to unconscious identification and the related phenomena of *participation mystique,* a clarification of those terms will be provided in the following.

3.2.2.1. Identification, Projection, Transference and Mystical Participation

Giving a definition of *identification*, Jung writes,

> [Identity] is a characteristic of the primitive mentality and the real foundation of *participation mystique*, which is nothing but a relic of the original non-differentiation of subject and object, and hence of the primordial unconscious state. It is also a characteristic of the mental state of early infancy, and, finally, of the unconscious of the civilized adult. (Jung 1971, par. 741).

In other words, total unconscious identification amounts to the all-one of the archaic state. What psychologists, anthropologists and researcher of religion have termed *participation mystique* when they met people who not only held animistic notions, but also reported of soul-sharing with plants, rocks, or animals, can thus be described in terms of more particularistic identification belonging to the point-like unity of the magic consciousness. In this line Jung writes:

> [Participation mystique] consists in the fact that the subject cannot clearly distinguish himself from the object but is bound to it by a direct relationship which amounts to partial identity. . . . Among civilized peoples it usually occurs between persons, seldom between a person and a thing. In the first case it is a transference relationship . . . . In the second case there is a similar

influence on the part of the thing, or else an identification with a thing or the idea of a thing (Ibid. par. 781).

In an again different place Jung explains that *differentiation* is the characteristic of consciousness, while non-differentiation is the original state of unconsciousness (Jung 1966, 206). Thus, everything that happens unconscious proceeds on the basis of non-differentiation – which means there is no determining whether it belongs or does not belong to oneself. Non-differentiation can lead to, or manifest itself as, mystical participation, where one for instance might experience a certain tree to contain ones soul (or sharing soul with a magpie), but also to the process of projection, which I use in the psychological self-defense mechanistic sense, denoting the (unconscious) act of transferring own feelings, emotions or impulses, which for instance stand in conflict with one's norms and values, onto another person, group or object in the external world[39]. Thus, if I was particularly arrogant, without being conscious of this circumstance, I might develop un-proportionally strong emotions against someone whom I experience as arrogant, since I might be projecting my own arrogance onto this person. Since the individuation-process in Jungian psychology is basically about integrating unconscious and undeveloped parts of the personality, the removal of projections is central to every psychological development in this frame. Projections are of course a hindrance for balanced relationships in general, and the removal thus crucial for every peace work.

The same goes for transference, a term that sometimes is used synonymous with projection, and denotes similar dynamics. Transference here denotes the projection of own, often unconscious, feelings and emotions, but especially also expectations and earlier experiences, especially from childhood, onto new circumstances and relationships. As such is it a very normal phenomenon, which often first becomes problematic when those transferences do not fit the new circumstances. For instance, if a young man were used to his mother preparing food and cleaning the house, he might get problems with his spouse, when he lives in 2014 and projects the role his mother used to have onto his spouse, and her expectation are contrary to his. Other examples might be to mistrust someone who resembles another in voice; manner or appearance, with someone one once had negative experiences with. For instance, if I have been beaten up by a bald-headed man, I might transfer this experience onto the next bald-headed man I meet, and become scared and unable to see the person for who he is, due to my by transference clouded awareness. I might likewise be unproportionally compliant towards a stranger, who resembles an old friend of mine. As such,

39 The reversed dynamic of projection is termed introjection and describes the process of undifferentiated (in other words unconscious) import from the external world into the internal (Cf. Dietrich 2011, 67).

unconscious transferences and projections denotes those dynamics by which the consciousness is clouded in its awareness of the world and oneself – it is the projection of one's own inner psychic content onto an external other context. Since they naturally also are the root of much (if not most) conflict(s), the conscious handling, working with, and the deconstruction of own and others projections and transferences is thus crucial to every kind of peace-worker and peace work – and general consciousness development and psychological maturing in life.

Another reason for mentioning these psychological processes of identification, transference and projections, is that 'seeing' SEs often easily and mistakenly are discharged as constituting instances of those unconscious processes. When I for instance look out the window and recognize how a flock of grey-geese who fly past symbolically most profoundly reflect my inner-psychic process, both in what the goose symbolizes in itself, the formation they fly in, as well as the number of geese, then the suspicion that I am somehow projecting my own inner-psychic state onto the scene and constructing the meaning-connections myself immediately suggests itself. This, however, is per definition not an instance of projection, mystical participation or pre-personal regress in the strict psychological sense, since those occur unconsciously and exactly do not differentiate between subject and object, inside and outside - the world and me. If this were the case I would not notice the fusion, equal to the egocentric child who does not understand that others can see it. The reason that Jung and others, including myself, are startled about seeing symbolical coincidences between inner states and outer happenings (in other words synchronicity) is exactly because we come from a dualistic mental ego-consciousness where we (more or less) clearly differentiate between subject and object – inside and outside – what is me, and what is not me. Because I mentally differentiate between the world and me and have learned to rationally analyze processes as causal movement through space and time, I do on the one hand not expect to see non-causal correspondences between the world and me and normally do not even have a term for it – and thus get startled when they occur[40]. On the other hand, I also do not give up my mental and rational differentiation through acknowledging synchronicity, because I still clearly differentiate between me as an integrated subject in space and time, with my own causal lines that connect me chronologically in the moment to the past and the future – and the outside object in space and time with its own causal lines and chronology. Acknowledging

[40] This is the reason some authors have treated synchronicity as „trickster "-phenomena, arguing how synchronicities function as a form of joker, shaking up too rational worldviews (for instance Combs & Holland (1991): „Through the eyes of science, myth, and the trickster: Synchronicity "). Obviously synchronicities can only function as jokers in those particular worldviews where they are unexpected, while they function differently in others.

synchronicity simply means to add (or rather re-discover) another layer of meaning between the two causally unrelated events. A quality of Kairos is added to the quantity of Kronos. The synchronicity-concept does thus not interfere with the causality-concept, or with other rational quantification and explanations. This is what Arthur Schopenhauer has in mind, when he states:

> All developments in the life of a human being would accordingly stand in two fundamentally different types of connections: first, in the objective, causal connection of the course of nature; second, in a subjective connection which exists only in relationship to the individual who experiences it and which is thus just as subjective as his own dreams, in which however, the succession and content are just as necessarily determined and in the same manner as the succession of scenes of a drama cast by a poet. That both types of connections exist simultaneously and the same occurrence, as a link in two quite different chains, which nevertheless have aligned perfectly in the consequence of which each time the fate of one matches the fate of another, and each is made the hero of his own drama while simultaneously figuring in an alien drama. This is freely also something that exceeds our powers of comprehension and can only be conceived as possible through the most fabulous preordained harmony (Schopenhauer 1922, 264-265).

Since Schopenhauer, in accord with his time, believes in absolute determinism, he has to assume a Leibnitzian 'preordained harmony' in order to explain the meaning-connections, which he describes as parallel-circles connecting the as meridians conceptualized causal-chains in what he terms a concurrent-relation (Ibid. 267). While the belief in absolute determinism literally has lost its ground since the findings of quantum-physics and their formulation of probability-fields, the proverbial apple that is said to have inspired Newton to his gravity-theory still falls close to the tree. This means that while Schopenhauer´s preordained harmony in many ways is obsolete, he still has to be credited with seeing and pointing to an ontological fundamental area, for which there are no *ad hoc* solutions.

Since synchronistic experiences per definition have a personal conscious component, towards which an extra dimension of meaning is added, they in accord with the earlier developed perspective and in relation to Wilber´s pre/trans fallacy definitely do not constitute a pre-personal regress, but rather a trans-personal plus. We only speak of synchronicity, since we have two synchronous, meaningfully related events – on one side the inner-psychic event of an integrated personal consciousness, and on the other side an outside meaningfully relating event – and not a free-floating diffuse oneness. Infantile or unconscious narcissism does not consciously differentiate this way, but simply takes for granted. As such, albeit a bit flat and provocative, I could state that the only difference between two persons seeing and recognizing the same coincidence, where one acknowledges and interprets a meaningful, literally trans-personal, connection, and the other interprets the same connection as mere chance, is that the former's interpretation is more meaning-full, whereas the latter is meaning-less. The question then is; *what do synchronistic events mean?* Or: *How can they be interpreted?*

In order to understand the Jungian perspective on the meaning-fullness of synchronicity and how they are to be interpreted, there are two more concepts that are crucial for an understanding. The first is *compensation,* and the other is the *individuation-process.*

3.2.3. Compensation

As argued above, psychologically normally unconscious phenomena such as identification, mystical participation and transferences are used creatively and purposefully in shamanism and traditional healing practices; however, as also indicated, such practices can indeed be dangerous and are traditionally surrounded by a lot of taboo and rules, and reserved for the experts (e.g. shaman or priest). Just as hypnotic suggestions contemporarily are also used for desired purposes (as for instance to stop smoking or change eating habits), the general (and indeed healthy) goal is to get rid of (hypnotic) introjections. Not only can the history of modern humanistic discourses be read as a history of deconstructing historically inherited introjections, and building new, presumably more reasonable doctrines; but as outlined above, psychological growth and consciousness development consists in differentiation between me and not me by simultaneous de-centering of the personal reference-frame. The key word for Jung when dealing with archetypes is consequently *vigilance*. Identifying with or getting possessed by an archetype is as pathological (or regressive) a reaction for the total psyche as is ignoring or repression. The Jungian idea(l) is to consciously mediate between the unconscious content which comes up as emotions, ideas, dreams and fantasies on the one hand, and the ego-consciousness on the other hand, until a third, transcendent to the former, and once again balanced, position is reached. This process is called *integration*, while the activity of the unconscious is understood as *compensatory*.

To recapitulate, it was argued how personal complexes and neurosis could express themselves symbolically in abnormal behavior or pains – but especially also in dream-pictures. In Jung´s understanding such symptoms can be read as 'messages' from the unconscious to the consciousness, addressing an imbalance of the ego-consciousness, with the purpose of establishing once again a harmonious balance - in system-theoretical terminology one would say *homeostasis*. Jung termed this process by which the unconsciousness outbalances one-sidedness of the consciousness compensation (sometimes also complementation). If for instance, a person would have an inferiority complex, the unconsciousness might typically compensate through dream pictures of being a king or queen, ruling and subduing other people - while people who have unrealistic or too high an opinion about themselves might dream of flying or falling (Jung 1964, 50). These particular examples of compensatory pictures would simultaneously also be complementary – the unconscious, however, which has to be regarded as an autonomous Thou in relation to the consciousness – is not simply complementary to the consciousness, but might as well conduct neutrally, if “satisfied” with the conscious content, or underpin an for instance dark mood with even darker content, after the principle “like curing like” (Ibid.). If the individual manages to integrate the unconsciously compensating material, they become part of the consciousness, which consequently expands and grows. This personal psychological growth and maturing process in the long term, however, is not random or aiming at an immediate fixed balanced state. By following series of dreams over longer time periods, Jung also detected larger patterns of compensatory activity that are not addressed at the immediate needs of the individual, but are facilitating a larger comprehensive development of the personality (Jacobi 1978, 127). Thus, Jung maintains that the psyche is not only a self-regulating system, capable of bringing about its own equilibrium, but also of bringing about its own self-realization. This process of self-realization Jung calls the *individuation-process,* which is central to Jung´s psychology as a whole.

3.2.4. Individuation

With the individuation-process, I have simultaneously reached Jung´s psychology of religion. The term self-realization has in the context of individuation to be taken quite literally, which means it is the self that seeks to realize itself. What Jung termed the self is however not identical with the earlier described self in reference to Wilber and Dietrich, but with the soul for Emerson and Gebser, which becomes a direct conscious experience at the integral structure. Jung identified the self as the central, unifying archetype. It is the point of orientation and meaning for the psyche as a whole, the archetype around which all the other are grouped and ordered (Jacobi 1978, 44). Jung described the self as the archetype whose centre is everywhere and whose circumference is nowhere, explaining that its phenomenology cannot be distinguished empirically from a God-image (Combs and Holland 1990, 121). It is here that Jung´s psychology becomes religious, at least in the sense of *religare*; here meaning 'bound back on' this central archetype. The individuation process is arguably also spiritual in the sense of the expanding consciousness during the process. Through the process of compensation the self, through the symbol, does “all the time urge us to overcome our unconsciousness,” which is no easy task, since “[h]uman nature has an invincible dread of becoming more conscious of itself,” but “the Self demands sacrifice by sacrificing itself to us” (Jung 1990b, 263).

The Jungian analytic Robert Atziz means that the latter is an especially important notion, since it draws attention to an often overlooked aspect of the ego-self relationship.

> Great attention is usually given to the sacrifice made by the ego as it struggles to integrate the compensatory material with which it is presented. We tend, however, to overlook the fact that the self too is making a sacrifice, as it works, through the symbol, to express itself in the more limiting world of the ego (Atziz 1990, 21).

In other words, in Jung´s perspective the self is both the source and the goal of psychic development, the archetype that from the very beginning has served as "the *secret spiritus rector* of our fate." (Jung 1978, 70). While this has obvious teleological implications, it is indeed agreeing with the earlier outlined systematic of consciousness development, where the self was described as awaken to dream-like consciousness in the mythic structure, suppressed in the mental ego formation and becoming conscious in the integral observation – only made possible through the prior formation of mental ego-consciousness. Noteworthy already here is that Jung advocates a conscious integration of the self into ego-awareness – or put on its head, an integration of ego-consciousness into the wider awareness of the self – and not a resolution into pre-egoic states of consciousness, which is what Wilber accuses Jung of. Another point to be made is, since the compensatory activity, which both facilitates the immediate needs as well as the comprehensive development of the personality, is situated in and comes from the unconscious itself, it derives that the ego is not the instance that chooses its goal, but rather is led by the unconscious to it. This further implies, that the only productive course of action for the individual is to move along with the current of this comprehensive process (Atziz 1990, 18).

Exemplary, the Buddhist and Hindu concept of enlightenment becomes in the Jungian symbolical understanding synonymous with the Christian mystical *unio mystica* and the alchemical 'hieros gamos of the soul,' describing the state (or moment) when the 'light of consciousness' is united (or wedded) with and shining through the former dark underworld of the unconsciousness (Jung 1952, 48). I can now add that this in a transrational sense simultaneously means a disclosure of the former unconscious 'overworld' - the higher layers of the matrix. Jung describes the experience of the ego-self relationship at the end of the individuation in Christian terms, when he uses Paul's word "not I live now, but Christ lives through me" as a metaphor (see Ibid. 163). This clearly contains the famous ego-death motive, when Paul states "not I live now," which becomes even more visible when the whole sentence is taken in consideration, where Paul states: "I have been crucified with Christ. Not I live now, but Christ lives through me" (Galatians 2, 20). The idea(l) for Jung is thus not to identify with the Self (or with any other archetype for that sake), which in this case would be equal to saying "I am god," and cause a narcissist inflation, but to consciously serve and let the self, the inner light which in wholeness shines through the *persona*, live through oneself. Interestingly, when the Buddhist in the moment of enlightenment realizes Buddhahood - and not "the Buddha now lives through me" - this for Jung indicates that Buddhism, with its root in the much older Vedic tradition, sets of at a time when its people had not developed mental ego-consciousness, for which reason identification with the archetype of the self, of which the Buddha is a symbol for Jung, at this point is inevitable (Jung 152, 163).

In his book "*Psychology and Alchemy*" (1944) Jung parallels the alchemical goal of transforming lead into gold to the psychological process of individuation, proposing that the former alchemists were projecting their own unconsciousness symbolically into nature, and thus in fact were working on the same psychological individuation process. The same unification motif is analogous (or at least comparable) to the tantric goal of *Shiva* and S*hakti* unification, as well as to the rituals surrounding *Astarte* with *Adonis* for instance - and is as such finally grounded in the same energetic roots of which the transrational school of peace-studies is feeding – and shares the same goal of balancing and uniting opposites; for the various purposes of fertility, harmony and wholeness - arguably all related to, if not synonyms for, peace. The difference between energetic (archaic, magic and mythic) practices and trans-personal (and Jungian) oriented practice is then that the latter seek to consciously realize what the former did intuitively and spontaneously.

3.2.4.1. Preliminary Remarks on Jungian Psychology

With this Jungian concept of compensation and individuation, Jung grants emotions and their accompanying manifestations such as dreams, phantasies and psychosomatic effects a higher intrinsic value than other psychological schools, by placing them as reference frame at the center of psychological development and even ascribing them a teleological quality in their relationship with the ego-consciousness. As outlined Jung does not advocate to give oneself over to phantasies and emotions, but to consciously work on an (symbolic/mythological) understanding and integration of these motifs and emotions which come up and compensate the personality. In other words, Jungian psychology sets of at the rational mental ego-consciousness at the fourth chakra and searches to consciously advance into the material, which comes up from the lower chakras, especially in its mythological form of the third chakra, all the time balancing and harmonizing this material with the ego-consciousness. Since the mental layer of the ego-consciousness builds on those prior layers and is in a relationship of feedback-loops with these, it is reasonable to assume, or set up, a possible progressive dialectic between those layers - as Jung does. This, however, also suggests that what the Jungian analytical process does is uncovering and differentiating the mythical structure in its meaningfulness for the personal life – and not advancing into the spiritual, trans-personal layers as formulated by the transrational perspective. This suspicion is further borne out by Jung´s description of the self as an archetype, which implies that this self is bound up with emotional and symbolical qualities – and theoretically thus does not mean the same as the yogic and transrational Self, which as immovable and forever unborn Spirit, the Being-as-such, completely quality less. This would also give way to another explanation to the by Jung observed difference between the Buddhist enlightenment and the by Jung envisioned "enlightenment." Instead of the by Jung alleged pre-egoic consciousness structure of the historical Buddhists being responsible for their likewise alleged unconscious identification with the self in the moment of enlightenment, it could also be that Jung´s necessary adherence to the ego-consciousness while searching for spirituality and meaning in mythic dream-pictures inevitably leads Jung to a God-Image as center of the formerly unconscious psyche, and simultaneously inhibits him from going the way of the ego-death. Giving up the ego in this case would indeed lead to narcissistic inflation – while the Buddhist concept of enlightenment means something completely different than just experimentally knowing and consciously relating to the structure, condition and processes of the psyche. As precondition for enlightenment the Buddhist and yogi also examines unconscious processes (which thus become conscious), but only to own and master the formerly unconscious processes through ascetic exercises, in order to free him/herself from the profane human condition (in its 'enslavement' to the unconscious) and transcend towards spirit. For Jung the goal is never to master the unconscious, but on the contrary to listen carefully to its movements and let oneself be guided by it, through which the Jungian approach becomes a form of conscious, living mythology. While for Jung the unconscious thus constitutes the spring of meaning, and aim for the personal life, and is the center around which Jungian analysis revolves, the same unconsciousness constitutes for the yogi just another aspect of the worldly condition which one has to master in order to lay it behind forever. Jung almost involuntarily advocates to install a sort of internal observer in order to not identify with the unconscious material, and thus advances backwards into the integral structure, but cannot advance from there, with his eyes and mind fixed on the mythic structure from where the soul unfolds, which for him contain the meaning and aim of the personal life and thus constitute the center around which Jungian analysis revolves. The yogi on the other hand, who despises everything this- and other-worldly as essentially meaning suffering, searches to liberate him/herself from the cycle of perpetual becoming – a cycle towards which the Jungian archetypes certainly belong. The *purusa* (Spirit) of the Samkhya and Yoga tradition, which is free of every attribute and which is what the yogi searches to free from its entanglement with the world, means thus something quite different than the Jungian self.

In how far these different understandings of the Self diverge or after all coincide has already been discussed. For now it is important to note that Jung clearly is delving into the mythic structure of the unconscious and revolving around its complexes of motifs in search of meaning.

Due to the archetypes tendency to form symbols, it is according to Jung through the study and knowledge of symbols that the meaning of the unconscious 'messages' can be deciphered. Generalized magic and mythic consciousness in its concrete understanding of the world reads symbols and dream-pictures rather literally. For instance, when a man among the Kai people of New Guinea dreams that he has sexual intercourse with his friend's wife, he is punishable, because the dream constitutes a concrete reality, which often is considered even more real than everyday experiences (Cf. Levy-Bruhl 1923, 103-104). For Jung, who operates from a level of abstraction which clearly belongs to the mental layer, every dream-picture is a symbol which never has to be understood literally, but only as a metaphor or an allegory for something else. Dreaming about a friend's wife might thus symbolize one's own wife (and the friend might stand for oneself) or she might symbolize the anima or the like, but never the friend's actual wife. Since Jung thus in his work with dream-analysis always already were looking for symbolical correspondences, he was perfectly predisposed to actually see symbolical correspondences also outside the confines of his patients' and his own dreams and phantasies – and in consequence coin the term synchronicity. In the following I will take up some examples of synchronicity and explain how they are to be understood in a Jungian framework – and later on how this as feedback influenced Jung´s personal practice and theoretical outlook.

3.3. Synchronicity and Archetypes

When I together with Jung assume that the constellation of archetypes, as in unconscious semi-autonomous content with a highly emotional charge, is the determining factor in SE's, then it consequently follows that synchronicity forms part of the postulated compensatory relationship between the unconscious and the ego. Since this compensation also forms part of the individuation-process, it becomes understandable why Robert Mansfield has termed synchronicity poetically as “soulmaking in action” (Mansfield 1995, 27). Here, I agree with Robert Atziz that one of the central points in the synchronicity theory is that nature, through the archetypes, compensates consciousness both inwardly and outwardly (Atziz 1990, 59). In this regard I also agree with Atziz, when he further differentiates Jung´s initial definition and states that the compensatory activity of the archetype not necessarily has to be experienced both inwardly and outwardly (Ibid.). Hence, in the Jungian framework there are two major kinds of synchronistic experience; one where the compensatory activity of the archetype is experienced both inwardly and outwardly, and secondly one where the compensatory activity is experienced outwardly only. With these theoretical preparations I will in the following examine some case-examples, which along the way as well will exemplify Jungian analysis.

3.3.1. Synchronicity in Action

Jung´s arguably most famous example of synchronicity is the subtle case of the "golden scarab." Jung relates that this example concerns a young female patient, whose strongly rational attitude and education made every therapeutic endeavor very difficult.

> After several fruitless attempts to sweeten her rationalism with a somewhat more human understanding, I had to confine myself to the hope that something unexpected and irrational would turn up, something that would burst the intellectual retort into which she had sealed herself. Well, I was sitting opposite her one day, with my back to the window, listening to her flow of rhetoric. She had had an impressive dream the night before, in which someone had given her a golden scarabeus costly piece of jewelry. While she was telling me this dream, I heard something behind me gently tapping on the window. I turned round and saw that it was a fairly large insect that was knocking against the window-pane from outside in the obvious effort to get into the dark room. This seemed to me very strange (since insects normally fly towards light, <A/N>). I opened the window immediately and caught the insect in the air as it flew in. It was a scarabaeid beetle or common rose-chafer (Cetonia aurata), whose gold-green colour most nearly resembles that of a golden scarab. I handed the beetle to my patient with the words, "Here is your scarab." This experience punctured the desired hole in her rationalism and broke the ice of her intellectual resistance. The treatment could now be continued with satisfactory results (Jung 1969, 525-526).

Besides Jung´s remarkable apprehension, this case has many more intriguing implications. As Jung points out, any essential change of attitude signifies a psychic renewal, which is usually accompanied by rebirth-symbols in the respective persons dreams and fantasies. The scarab is exactly such a classic rebirth-symbol, appearing in the Egyptian "Book of What is in the Netherworlds," where the dead sun-god changes himself at the tenth station into Khebri, the scarab, before he at the twelfth station mounts the barge which carries him rejuvenated into the morning sky – a fact that most likely was unknown to the young woman (Ibid. 439). If I trust Jung´s assessment of the young woman's situation, it can be noticed how the dream-picture fitted the compensatory needs of her ego-consciousness and simultaneously was a precognition of what was to come about the next day, which constitutes the first synchronistic event. This event, though, is delicately interwoven and overlaps with the second synchronistic event, which occurs when the beetle has its entrance, *synchronous* with the young woman speaking about the earlier scarab jewelry of her dream. Unfortunately Jung himself did not comment further on this particular case, except stating that it stands paradigmatically for innumerable cases of meaningful coincidence that have been observed by Jung and others, and are recorded in large collections (Ibid. 526).

However, with reference to the above and other similar cases, Jung states that SE´s consist of two factors: (1) an unconscious picture comes directly (literally) or indirectly (symbolized or indicated) to the consciousness as dream, idea or hunch, and (2) with this content coincides an objective event (Jung 1990, 36). As argued above SE´s, when understood as archetypal compensatory activity, do not necessarily need the coincidence of a parallel subjective and objective event, but can also be just an outside event or the coincidence of opposite or otherwise meaningfully relating content (Atziz 1990, 59). In other words, the archetypes working in the unconscious (or just emotions in general), can manifest themselves in objective events without necessarily simultaneously as well trespassing into the consciousness of the subject from within. While this claim opens up for fascinating possibilities, for instance that the subjective experience of the outside world indeed always already could be a perfect mirror of the inside, which would set the ancient paradigm of "microcosm equal macrocosm" in a quite concrete perspective, such relations are obviously even harder to prove and verify inter-subjectively, and opens up for even stronger self-referentiality. Once again, the subject should indeed know what belongs to her and what does not, that is to say, in the Jungian frame one should be able to separate the specific compensatory value of the object from what the object is in itself. When one begins to identify with the synchronistic patterning around oneself, and does not differentiate between subject and object, or just projects own delusions into the happening, pathology lures just around the corner.

> Since archetypal situations are not uncommon in schizophrenia, we must also suppose that corresponding synchronistic phenomena will occur which follow exactly the same course as with so -called normal persons. The difference lies simply and solely in the interpretation. The schizophrenic´s interpretation is morbidly narrow because it is mostly restricted to the intentions of other people and to his own ego-importance. The normal interpretation... is based on the philosophic premise of the sympathy of all things, or something of that kind... If synchronicities occur in these cases it is because an archetypal situation is present, for whenever archetypes are constellated we find manifestations of the primordial unity. Thus the synchronistic effect should be understood not as a psychotic but as a normal phenomenon (Adler and Jaffé 1975, 409).

Marie-Louise von Franz gives an example, of a man who were projecting his own delusions of grandeur into a synchronistic phenomenon. The case involved a man who, on the verge of a psychotic breakdown, attacked his wife, who in turn called the police and a doctor. When they arrived at the scene and entered the house with the intention of forcibly removing the man to a clinic, the lamp in the corridor shattered with a bang, so that suddenly they were all standing in darkness in the midst of the broken glass (Franz 1980b, 196).

> The patient saw clearly that what had happened was a supernatural sign: just as the sun grew dark when Christ was crucified, this event was to him a confirmation that he was a savior who was being unjustly arrested. We, on the other hand, would say that he had projected his own delusion into the event. Thus the synchronistic phenomenon, in itself meaningful, was instead covered by a projection. To a person with normal consciousness the "meaning" of the occurrence would be quite different. A lamp, in contrast to the sun, is not a cosmic principle but an appliance invented by man; it usually symbolizes ego-consciousness in dreams and fantasies. The meaning of the unusual event would then more probably be expressed thus: In the moment of intense agitation caused by his imminent arrest the patient's ego-consciousness was shattered and a "mental blackout" resulted. The patient, however, could not grasp this meaning (Ibid. 197).

While this example again demonstrates how the outside events, the shattering of the lamp, synchronistically reflect the inner-psychic events of the man in a compensatory meaningful way, it also demonstrates how own ego-importance can obscure the interpretation of SE´s – and gives an example of Jungian interpretation (a lamp symbolizing ego-consciousness). When such archetypal manifestations are misinterpreted and/or not consciously integrated, the emotional affect in which the man finds himself (Jung would probably speak of an archetypal possession) might take hold and trigger more synchronistic events in the same line, which again, misunderstood in the same initial way can establish a chronically condition, where the synchronistic phenomena around the person become self-fulfilling prophecies. An example of this kind is related by Surprise:

> I had a client who suffered from paranoid delusions. He was sure he was being followed by undercover government agents all the time. He said he saw them watching him everywhere. He had no idea why they were so interested in him, but he was sure he was being watched. In a session one afternoon, he was telling me all about it. I tried to convince him nobody was watching him, that there was nothing to be afraid of. I asked him to come to the office window overlooking the street. I challenged him to point out the people who were watching him. At that moment a car drove by with two men in it. Both stared directly at the window we were looking out of as the car slowly passed. "You see!" my client exclaimed. "There they are, right there!" I have no idea what those men were actually doing. Maybe they were looking for an address. Maybe they were interested in the building itself. They weren't spies. My client had a diagnosis of paranoid schizophrenia. He had been ill for many years. He had a paranoid delusion of being followed, but the synchronistic events that flowed from it were real. He was looking into the reflection caused by his own illness. I was not able to help him. He did not have the ability to step outside his belief in the truth of his own thoughts. I didn't know how to give it to him (Surprise 2012, 56).

This example demonstrates clearly what Jung has in mind when calling the schizophrenic´s interpretation morbidly narrow restricted to other people's intention and own ego-importance. Along this line, Atziz identifies three pathological or delusive reactions to synchronistic events: first, the tendency of the subject to enter into a type of *participation mystique* with the object, which means not to differentiate between the compensatory import or symbolical meaning of the object for the subject, and what the object is in itself (as among other was the case in Surprise´s example with the patient with paranoid delusion); secondly, to misinterpret the compensatory meaning of the synchronistic event, such as was the case in von Franz´s example, where the patient incorrectly interpreted the shattering of the lamp denoting that he was an unjustly arrested savior like Christ; and thirdly, to interpret synchronistic events as a manifestation of one´s or other individual´s personal power (Atziz 1990, 191). These by Atziz stated observations are correct - within a Jungian framework. When SE´s happen in connection with the constellation of an archetype, and the ego-consciousness cannot control the autonomous constellation, but in the best case does not identify with, and is not overwhelmed by the emotions, and in further steps consciously try to grasp the meaning of the archetype and integrate this meaning in one´s life, then SE´s are not manifestations of one´s or other individuals personal power. Then they are manifestations of the power of the collective unconscious. When archetypal manifestations have to be interpreted correctly in order to determine their compensatory value for a conscious integration, then SE´s, as one form of archetypal manifestations, also have to be interpreted correctly, and in the same way as for instance dreams. Finally, if one does not want to regress psychologically into archaic, magic or mythic fusion, both in the Jungian as well as in the above outlined sense, one should abstain from entering into identification with the surroundings but stay vigilant, and at all times differentiate between subject and object, inside and outside. This latter point, which on a first glance seems to be the simplest fallacy to avoid, can practically be quite problematic because of the mind's ability to match patterns.

The human brain's ability to match patterns in a complex, changing and uncertain environment is something every computer scientist dreams about being able to replicate. As such, everybody can see SE´s and normally begins seeing them as soon he or she starts looking for them. The reason we normally do not see SE´s is because we are cultivated to disregard such connections, and in our dominant mental mode are caught up in a fundamental dualism between subject and object. Due to the mind's ability to match pattern and construct, often less meaningful narratives from those patterns, for instance conspiracy theories are booming. However, even with a critical approach to knowledge, when one begins to see SE´s and look in this direction for connections (and given that the interpretation is not obscured by own ego-importance or the alleged intentions of others, as in many obscure conspiracy theories), the mind's ability to match the pattern between inner emotions and outer events is most astonishing. Especially when taking the possibility of unconscious emotions as well being reflected into consideration. Then the possibility that the entire range of my inner state constantly is symbolically reflected in the outside world comes to mind – and eventually an experience. If this thought and/or experience is comprehended one can share Schopenhauer´s astonishment about how wonderfully this world is made, when this complete reflection is valid for every single subjective experience of the world all the time. Such visions do not only lead the associations towards a most wonderfully arranged All-One or the old Vedic formula of atman=Brahman, but also into a rather comprehensive solipsism or mystical participation. Jung was surely conscious of such dangers, as well as the academically orthodox judgment about such theories and experiences, for which reason he only validated something as an instance of synchronicity when the event was so strong that it could be inter-subjectively checked – as for instance when Louis XIV of France´s great watch breaks and stops in the moment of his death[41]. Such events, then, would typically be the case in those emotionally intense situations in which, according to Jung, constellations of archetypes are involved, while the potential synchronicity between not much going on inside me and not much is going on around me is disregarded as meaningless. If, however, synchronicity as a principle would denote the symbolical reflection of all emotions, it would still clearly be the strong and accumulated states, which would be the most obvious. That Jung´s personal experience and considerations probably due to this tendency as well went into a more encompassing vision and application of the principle of synchronicity is not only suggested by Jung´s postulation of synchronicity as a principle equal and complementary to causality. In the following I will therefore outline and conclude the further consequences of the synchronicity-concept for Jung and his work, and demonstrate how central the synchronicity-concept was for Jung, before concluding this work by discussing Jung´s concept of synchronicity in a transrational perspective.

3.3.2. The Consequences of Synchronicity

In regard to Jung´s theory of the archetypes, his work and reasoning can grossly be divided in two periods and movements; the early period where Jung via dream-analysis and his discovery of the collective unconscious basically saved all of the worlds mythologies from "enlightened" ridicule by the academic establishment, through placing all the gods and goddesses of the heavens and all demons and demonesses of the hells inside the human psyche as more or less autonomous archetypes residing in the collective unconscious. From there the gods and goddesses would continue to do what they always have done; structure the emotions, dreams, spontaneous ideas and creativity of the humans, and in this way influence their fate. With his formulation of the Self as central and unifying archetype, which encompasses all the other archetypes, Jung managed to syncretize this 'inner polytheism' with a more Christian monotheism, where the work of all the other archetypes in the end act as servants and aspects of the

[41] Watches stopping in the moment of their owner's death are a rather often-witnessed phenomenon.

one inner self/god. The theoretical formulation that all the gods of heaven and hell are projections of inner-psychic phenomena is contemporarily one of the paradigms on which transpersonal psychology rests (Cf. Dietrich 2008, 383).

The second movement of the late Jung is much less known, since he never wrote much publicly on the consequences of his synchronicity-theory for his own work and practice. However, clear is that through the formulation of his synchronicity-hypothesis, Jung assumes that the archetypes as well manifest outside of the human psyche, by which they are no longer confined to the psyche but rather become "transgressive" agents. Interesting and revealing in this regard is a letter of Jung´s dated July 10, 1946, where he writes to his correspondent:

> Your view that the collective unconscious surrounds us on all sides is in complete agreement with the way I explain it to my pupils. It is more like an atmosphere in which we live than something that is found in us... Also, it does not by any means behave merely psychologically; in the cases of so-called synchronicity it proves to be a universal substrate present in the environment rather than a psychological premise. Wherever we come into contact with an archetype we enter into relationship with transconscious, metapsychic factors which underlie the spiritualist hypothesis as well as that of magic actions (cited after Atziz 1990, 177).

In the here implied theoretical shift, Jung leaves behind a 'psychologization' of mythology and enters a full-blown *mythic* psychology and consciousness. With his description of archetypes being "transconscious, metapsychic factors," the gods and spirits of old are once again seen as invisible forces operating space and time transcending in and outside of the human. As such Martin Buber´s bitter critique of Jung can be refuted. Buber, who criticized Jung of religious reductionism, wrote:

> If religion is a relation to psychic events, which cannot mean anything other than to events of one own´s soul, then it is implied by this that it is not a relation to a Being or Reality which, no matter how fully it may from time to time descend to the human soul, always remains transcendent to it. More precisely, it is not the relation of an I to a Thou (Buber, 1957; 79).

By now it is clear that Jung ultimately came to view religious content not as rising from a strict intra-psychic ground, but from a "universal substrate present in the environment," in other words the psychoid archetype, which manifests in nature as well as in the psyche. With this significant theoretical step, Jung is carried beyond his earlier projectionism of a strict intra-psychic model and finds himself face to face with that transcendent Thou, the transcendent 'Reality' to which Buber refers. In his later writings regarding the archetype of the self in its form as both intra-psychic and metaphysical factor, Jung thus writes:

> We know from experience that it has long been there and is older than the ego, and that it is actually the "secret spiritus rector" of our fate. The self does not become conscious by itself, but has always been taught, if at all, through a tradition of knowing (the "purusha/atman" teaching, for instance)... the self, moreover, is an archetype that invariably expresses a situation within which the ego is contained. Therefore, like every archetype, the self cannot be localized in an individual ego-consciousness, but acts like a circumambient atmosphere to which no definite

limits can be set, either in space or in time. (Hence the synchronistic phenomena so often associated with activated archetypes) (Jung 1978, 167 – 168).

I agree with Atziz assessment that as an intra-psychic factor the self is for Jung the *atman*, in other words the 'ultimate discovered introspectively,' while the self as metaphysical principle is to be sure equivalent to *Brahman*, in other words, the ultimate as discovered objectively' (Atziz 1990, 183). As such develops Jung´s psychology to something akin to a monistic philosophy much in line with the Advaita Vedanta[42]. The personal soul (atman/self) is thus seen and understood as identical with the World-Soul (Brahman).

In Jung´s panentheistic vision the World-Soul thus rises from the *Unus Mundus,* the psychoid unitary background, and splits into the dynamic and complementary pair of instinct and spirit, where instinct stands for the material, causal and energetic aspect of Being and spirit for the invisible, synchronistic and passive *meaning* of Being. Jung, who used the terms God, Tao, the Great Spirit etc. interchangeable, refers to Wilhelm´s translation of the Tao Te King, in explaining the relation between Tao and meaning. In chapter eleven Lao Tzu states;

"Thirty spokes unite around one hub to make a wheel. It is the presence of the empty space that gives the function of a vehicle. Clay is molded into a vessel. It is the empty space that gives the function of a vessel. Doors and windows are chisel out to make a room. It is the empty space in the room that gives its function. Therefore, something substantial can be beneficial. While the emptiness of void is what can be utilized." (Lao Tzu, Tao Te King)[43]

Jung comments that the "empty space," the *Tao*, in other words (and translations) the "Nothing," obviously is what gives *meaning* and is called "no-thing" because it does not exist in the world of senses, but only acts as its *ordering* principle (Jung, 1990, 66). God, Tao or Brahman are here understood as equal to *meaning.* The identity between atman and Brahman (or personal soul and World-Soul) is thus for Jung a synchronistic, space and time transcending coincidence of *meaning*. This means, it is the same *meaning,* which manifests as personal self within the person – and from the perspective of the person manifests synchronistically as God or Brahman in the World. The reason every person simultaneously has a unique and individual *meaning,* that there exist a myriad of meanings, is then of course due to the persons (and all other entities) simultaneous different placement and perspectives in time and space. For describing this particular relationship between individuality and universality I

[42] My question regarding the relation between Jung´s psychology and transrational philosophy is in many ways thus a contemporary version of the ancient discussion and dialog between disciples of the Upanishad and the schools of thought following the Samkhya system.

[43] Quoted after www.Taoism.net and *Tao Te Ching: Annotated & Explained*, published by SkyLight Paths in 2006.

could also borrow Dietrich´s term of the *polymorphous pax universalis* (Cf. Dietrich 2008, 375). Because my soul coincides with the World-Soul prior to time and space I am one with everything – and can experience pre-cognitive dreams and other SE´s. Because I have a consciousness in time and space I also have a unique perspective, meaning and individuality in relation to all other entities in space and time and the All-One.

If the personal self/soul and the World-Soul, probably that which transrational terminology calls the spirit of the planetary system (Cf. Dietrich 2008, 370-372), thus coincide, and the World-Soul synchronistically reflects the personal self from the personal perspective in time and space, it follows that a complete functional emergence of the self would amount to a full-blown synchronistic experience. To get even more to the heart of it, it follows that every person always already is having a full-blown synchronistic experience – and the reason that a person normally not is conscious of this circumstance, is among other reasons due to the circumstance that the archetype of the self (and so much other outward synchronistically perfectly reflected inner-psychic content) normally is unconscious. Once again Jung´s psychology can be understood in terms of Advaita Vedanta, where the goal of the individuation-process is to realize the always already existing coincidence of self and God - atman and Brahman. The Jungian process of integrating unconscious material amounts then to the *Tat tvam asi* of the Vedanta, the realization that "also this am I" (Jung would probably say, "also this is my self," differentiating between ego and self). The Jungian 'enlightenment,' the moment when the "light of consciousness shines through the former dark unconscious," which I have argued amounts to a conscious experience of the coincidence of atman and Brahman, self and World-Soul, and in Jung´s perspective would be experienced as full-blown SE, would then arguably as well constitute a case of paradoxical flowing into each other of intra-personal and inter-personal layers characteristic for the Witness awareness. In how far this full emergence of the self actually amounts to the Witness awareness in the transrational sense, I am soon in a position to discuss.

In accord with the system-theoretical doctrine of the-whole-determining-the-part (contrary to a reductionistic the-parts-determining-the-whole approach) Jung described the self/World Soul as all the time acting "secret spiritus rector" of our fate, pushing the ego towards more consciousness through its compensatory activity. Since this activity manifests both inside and outside, Jung could surely agree with the Samkhya sentence: "From Brahman to the last blade of grass, the Creation is for the benefit of spirit, until spirit has attained supreme knowledge" (Samkhya Sutra 3, 47, cited after Eliade 1982, 56). While this supreme knowledge for Jung would be in accord with Shankara´s Vedanta philosophy, denoting the conscious knowledge of formerly unconscious processes and eventually the coincidence of atman and Brahman reached through the compensatory activity of nature; Patanjali and other commentators of the Samkhya philosophy interpret this sentence as meaning that nature benefits the spirit by pushing the spirit to an understanding of its ontological difference to nature (Cf. Garbe 2013, 78), or by itself (nature) being part of the continuous suffering which it is to exist, thus helping the spirit to search liberation from existence, by constantly reminding the human of this suffering (Eliade 1977, 19). With these two different philosophical concepts of what self and spirit is, the difference between *purusha* and *atman*, for which Samkhya and Vedanta stand, and with the thereby implied different soteriological consequences, I could already initiate and anticipate a parallel running discussion of the relation between Jung´s synchronistic worldview and the transrational philosophy. However, my goal here is not to discuss parallels between Indian philosophy and different variations of humanistic and transpersonal psychology, but to understand Jung´s synchronicity-concept, and how its further implications are to be understood in relation to the earlier developed transrational diagram of consciousness development – and in how far synchronicity is a characteristic of transrational spirituality and the All-One. Towards this end I will in the following paragraph analyze how Jung applied SE´s in practice, and what this says about his characteristic relation to the diagram of transrational peace consciousness.

3.3.2.1. Acting on Synchronicity as Mythic Spirituality

It is no secret that Jung was very interested and conversant in divinatory methods such as the I Ching and for instance astrology[44], and at times probably would let himself be guided by those traditional systems. However, the question here is how Jung related to those more everyday synchronistic events, which Jung, due to his remarkable familiarity with the symbolical language of the unconscious – the language of synchronicity – was very sensitive towards, as the case of the golden scarabeus proves. In accord with Jung´s adherence to the mythic structure, constituted in his regard of the archetype of the self as both initiator and goal for psychological (and spiritual) development, and due to the coincidence of atman and Brahman, it consequently follows that Jung would take

44 Astrology is thus another way to either learn about one's microcosmic situation through the macrocosmic correspondence, or help one self or others to keep in "sync" with the macrocosm and predict changes. Interestingly, the astrologist Mellie Uyldert describes astrological correspondences as synchronistic and not causal influences (Uyldert 1990, 37-38). For instance, when a child has asthma, for Uyldert this is not caused by for instance an existing allergy against cat-hairs (physiological explanation) or because the child is unproportional afraid due to its strict parenting (psychological explanation) or because the house she lives in is to small (circumstances as explanation), but all these factors are expressions of a *synchronistic pattern* which express the same *theme*, in this case a theme which the astrologists terms Saturn (Ibid.).

pretty much everything as a compensatory message from the self towards the right direction for development, since he in the final analysis saw the whole world as manifestations of the wider Self towards which the inner self stands in a synchronistic relation. Robert Atziz can thus cite Barbara Hannah, a student and later colleague of Jung, relating that when Jung analyzed his patients in the 'garden room,' which was a small square room at the corner of his garden directly on a lake, he would take every natural event, such as insects flying in, the lake lapping more audibly than usual, and so on, as belonging synchronistically to what was being said in the analysis (Atziz 1990, 85). Atziz also points to the following case provided by Henry K. Fierz, based on a meeting Fierz had with Jung in the 1950´s. This account demonstrates how Jung would let his own actions be guided by what he considered synchronistic events. Fierz, who had been tasked to publish a book of a recently deceased scientist, had, at the request of his publishers, forwarded a copy of the manuscript to Jung for his evaluation. After Jung had had time to read the manuscript, an appointment for 5:00 pm was arranged in order to discuss publication. Describing the events of that meeting, Fierz writes:

> Jung had read the book and he thought that it should not be published, but I disagreed and was for publication. Our discussion finally got rather sharp, and Jung looked at his wristwatch, obviously thinking that he had spent enough time on the matter and that he could send me home. Looking at his watch he said: "When did you come?" I: "At five, as agreed." Jung: "But that´s queer. My watch just came back from the watchmaker this morning after a complete revision, and now I have 5:05. But you must have been here much longer. What time do you have?" I: "It´s 5:35." Whereon Jung said: "So you have the right time, and I the wrong one. Let us discuss the thing again." This time I could convince Jung that the book should be published (Atziz 1990, 86).

Clearly, Jung took the stopping (or just the wrong time) of his watch as synchronistic reflection of the inner events of the episode, from which he concluded that he was wrong and Fierz right. In other words, the stopping of the watch was for Jung thus a message from a higher (or rather deeper) intelligence (the self), telling him about the situation. As a consequence Jung altered his conscious attitude and began to support the publishing of the book, instead of being against it, as initially was the case. That Jung would act on such a synchronicity, that he would take the coincident stopping of his watch as the better knowledge compared to his conscious standpoint in regard to publishing, is only consequent considering Jung´s synchronistic worldview, where the all-knowing archetype of the Self causing those synchronicities is the focal point." In line with this goes Von Franz description of what she considered the specifically religious character of attending to the compensatory activities of nature as experienced both inwardly and outwardly – a practice she compares to the traditional Chinese idea of acting in harmony with Tao.

> Religion means never acting only in accordance with conscious reasoning, but with constant attention... [to] the unknown participating factors. For instance, if somebody says: "Let us have coffee together after the lecture," if I think only that I have time since I don't have lunch until 12:30, that would be conscious reasoning, which of course is also correct, but if I am a religious person, I will stop for a minute and try to get a feeling as to whether it is right to do that, and if I have an instinctive feeling against it, or at that moment a window bangs shut, or I stumble, then I might not go... [A]ll the time one should concentrate and try to get some signs from the Self... In Chinese philosophy, it is tantamount to paying constant attention to the Tao, whether what I am now doing is right, in Tao (Franz 1980c, 95).

That the Jungian synchronistic perspective is a mythic form of reasoning and interpreting the world - and not an integral or transpersonal form of spirituality - becomes in the above quote especially visible. In relation to my earlier developed perspective uses Von Franz the term religion correctly in this context. What commonly is termed religion, as argued earlier in this work, flows from the mythic layer, both in its form as intra-personal meaning-constituting, intelligent mythology and as an inter-personal community constituting factor. What Von Franz advocates is, just as Jung, exactly to stop and listen to the inner feelings (magic) and visions (mythic) or the therewith associated synchronistic events in the surroundings, and base decisions on those manifestations of those unconscious impulses. When "all the time one should concentrate and try to get some signs from the Self," then this is not an integral freedom and awareness of all layers including the mental, but revolves around the mythic layer of which the archetype of the self is the center - and applying ones mental capacities uncontrolled towards always reading those 'signs' and conducting accordingly.

There are two more characteristics I will mention, which clearly places the synchronistic model in the mythic consciousness structure. Firstly, the atman equal Brahman equation is a true child of the mythic structure in its ego-centrism - which in this context rather has to be called a self-centrism. The question and orientation for Jung and Von Franz when it comes to synchronicity is all the time: "what does that mean for me and my Self?" - or in the context of their analytical work; "what does that mean for my patient?" As such this self-centeredness can indeed be forgiven as an 'occupational hazard' in the case of Jung and Von Franz, just as the discovery of synchronicity as a constituting factor of the magic and mythic structure as well can be explained causally by the occupation of Jung. Meanwhile, this does not change the inherent self-centeredness and egocentric dynamic in relating outside events to inner-psychic conditions, as inevitably is the case in recognizing synchronicity and which also constitutive for mythic reasoning. This, then, leads me to the second unmistaken characteristic, which connects synchronicity to the mythic structure.

As outlined earlier in this work, mythic consciousness and reasoning are among others characterized as concrete operational, which means that the mind's operations work along concrete objects, which for instance is the case when one uses fingers and toes for counting - or worships the sun as God. Synchronicity now is arguably another form of concrete operational reasoning – even though it understands the concrete objects as symbols. As Von Franz points out, when the decision whether I will have coffee after lecture or not (or make a forceful intervention into a conflict) is based solely on abstract thoughts concerning my later schedule (or the hoped for outcome of an intervention) this is conscious reasoning – and I can add belonging to the mental layer while disregarding all other layers – and though not typical for modern decision making, it is the ideal of modern rationality. Mental rationality, just as ethical considerations, do not orientate along concrete, visible objects, but on imagined circumstances and outcomes, such as mathematical calculations ordering a schedule concerning the invisible future or the question "what would be if everybody would do this?" which then are transferred back onto the visible episode. Meanwhile, what Von Franz advocates, and Jung practices, is to take concrete objects existing in the here and now into consideration – whether as intra-personal feeling, but even more so when synchronistically relating to symbolical circumstances as the window shutting with a bang, the entrance of a certain insect, or the stopping of a watch. When I base my decision and understanding of what is right for me to do and "where my place is – where I am in Tao" on concrete objects, I am per definition in a concrete operational mode and moving in a mythic logic and consciousness. When reacting on synchronistic events, due to their connection with feelings and emotions and their character of point-like unity, one is in fact very close to a full-blown pre-operational, magic consciousness and modus.

This way of synchronistic, mythic interpretation and decision-making is in itself not wrong or inferior to for instance a rational based process. It is simply a different worldview with its own inherent logic, and even rationally sound conclusions based on empirical evidence. Depending on the perspective, it has its downsides compared to a formal operational modus, for instance in the form of its more limited freedom, but also advantages, for instance in its sporadic access to certain forms of knowledge that transcends by far the capacities of pure rationality. It is a worldview the Transrational School probably would term *energetic,* and I in the frame of this paper term *mythic.* However, coming back to the question whether to grab that coffee or not, Von Franz implies in my view correctly that mythic and rational based interpretations of the situation might come to completely different answers and thus act as mutually exclusive. The schedule tells my rational ego yes, but in the dropping pencil I hear another voice saying no. As such, this having to decide between either following unconscious guidance or rational calculus is definitively not a holistic, integrated act characteristic for the integral structure and transpersonal mode, but either a mental giving in to the advantage of the unconscious or a neglect of the unconscious – which both are not the most favorable scenarios. The internal observer through the observation, just as Jungian analysis, uncovers the deeper layers of the psyche and might also recognize synchronicity, but the observer does not make the observed the focal center of gravity – which is what Jung does. The observer is its own paradoxically subjectless center, which simply is.

What here come to the fore are two different understandings of the self; the difference between *atman* and *purusha*, soul and spirit – and the great confusion throughout history about those terms. Jung, the "*Seelenklempner,*" has always been engaged with the depths of the soul, the archetype of the self, this vast kingdom spanning the whole globe, and which is where the gods and goddesses whisper to the human and unfold their numinous enchantment. It is this wild and fertile jungle Jung roamed as a Western-pioneer, trying to learn about it for its own sake, only surviving by his wits and ego-strength. For the yogi on the other hand, getting to know the soul is only a means to an end – and this end is the complete liberation of the spirit from this living and suffering soul. When the yogi goes into her body and psyche, following every movement to its source, it is in order to master her body and soul, because the yogi knows that she only can liberate herself by her own will from something she masters – and not something she is servant to. This is something else than the mystical union, which Jung is seeking. Ascetic exercises are meant to forcefully kill and master life – not following the will and guidance of life. Indicative in this regard is also that the famous *siddhis,* those occult powers which basically are a number of ESP phenomena, and stand in connection with the archetype of the self, which the yogi attains and masters through his practice, are disregarded as worthless in themselves and have to be transcended for complete liberation (Eliade 1977, 99). The profane life is here revealed as an enslaved affair, something most people even are not aware of while they are busy living up to their social and biological conditioning and the urges and drives of the unconscious, believing the ideas in their heads are their own. The word *yoga* means translated exactly 'enslavement' - denoting the practice of liberation from life´s enslavement by 'enslaving' it oneself[45]. Just as with the earlier described difference between the magic and witness-awareness, the question is whether one rides the wave or gets ridden. Jung was surely a faithful servant of life who never searched liberation from it. He searched to uncover her secrets buried in the depth of the soul – and I believe he came further than most in this endeavor.

3.3.3. Fields of Knowledge

The circumstance alone to recognize SE´s constitutes thus a case of 'ego-enlightened' entering either to magic or mythic consciousness in its pre- or concrete operational self-referential and egocentric correlation between inside and outside – while whether it is more magic or mythic depends on the

[45] *Yoga* means literally yoke, which is used to 'enslave' oxen – while the oxen can be understood as symbol for nature and life.

interpretation whether the synchronistic event is understood as expressing a transgressive agent (Jung´s mythic interpretation) or one's own or others magic abilities. In both cases is it what transrational terminology would term an *energetic* understanding. Wilber´s opinion that Jung and his followers were not forwarded into trans-personal spheres, but regressed into pre-personal layers is thus partly correct. It is only partly correct, because Jung indeed with open eyes would work his way from a conscious ego-perspective into the mythic layer adopting an 'enlightened' mythic worldview, until he with his recognition of synchronicity was well into the magic layer and his theory of the psychoid archetype speculated about archaic modalities – all the time adhering to a mythic interpretation. Wilber is also wrong in the sense that his postulated trans-personal spheres do not lie beyond the archaic, magic, mythic and mental layers, but constitute modalities which only are established by also working through the mental, mythic, magic and archaic layers[46]. The difference between Jung and the yogic practice lies solely in the attitude and way of dealing with the unconscious. Where Jung searched to integrate the unconscious soul into ego-consciousness, the yogic and transrational way works by separating consciousness from the soul through killing the ego, which is the connecting link between the two. In both variations one has to know and work through the own unconscious.

In my reading and here presented interpretation of the material, I thus assume that the above described integral layer indeed can be termed trans-mythic, in that the withdrawal of the Observer indeed opens up for the Jungian archetypal self to emerge. The difference is that Jung from here on would use all his mental capacities to dwell into this World-Soul and make it the center of his individuation-process – while the Observer remains detached from this archetypal self and through the meditative observation both calms and eventually masters the unconscious, all the time centered in a complementary self which also shines through, and which is the subjectless consciousness of what I could term the spirit-self. While Jung used many years studying the mythic layer of the personality before he became so conversant with the magic manifestations of the psyche, which he termed synchronicity that he started to incorporate them into his theorizing, the yogi comparable spends lengths of time in the integral observation, aided by many other psychophysical exercises, before his ego is dissolved and the karmic seeds are burned up and he enters the Witness-awareness. The Witness-awareness then can indeed be termed trans-magic, in that it constitutes a conscious mastering of the magic layer.

---

46 See also the term Sanskrit term "*pratiloma*" which means "against the fur" and denotes the concept of consciously going back to the very origin of creation and thus reach the paradoxical unborn state and liberation from time (Eliade 1977, 193). It is also due to this practice that the yogi claims to re-call past lives.

As outlined above, the magic layer and consciousness are characterized by their connection to feeling and emotion, the point-like unity, the magic *pars pro toto*, where the consciousness in Gebser´s words is as "scattered all over the world." Due to Jung´s work regarding synchronicity and the archetypes some of these characteristics can now better be understood as field-phenomena. This is because synchronistic archetypal manifestations, where both subject and object are enveloped in a shared meaning-relation, suggest that knowledge, in its pre-rational and trans-rational variation, is more akin to field-phenomena in which both the perceiving subject and the external object are enclosed. In this context Erich Neumann has pointed out that the magic *participation mystique* incorrectly is explained as projection or exteriorization of a psychic condition (Neumann 1956, 86-87). When a so-called 'primitive' says he gets his knowledge from a bird that told him a secret, for which reason he calls it a doctor bird, the modern assumption is that the knowledge unconsciously already is 'in him,' but through the projection is experienced as coming from outside, while the connection to the bird is accidental. The more correct description of the situation, in light of the synchronicity-theory, would be that "the knowledge imparted to the primitive by means of the bird was a field knowledge, an extrane knowing, present or emerging in a living field wherein both bird and primitive are enclosed" (Ibid.). The magic pre-operational or mythic concrete operational characteristic of this event is that the respective person indeed gets his information from the outside bird – while he remains unconscious of the simultaneous emergence or presence of the same knowledge inside him. It is indeed as if the consciousness here is scattered all over the place, understanding and following information from, what in an ego-perspective has to be called, outside manifestations[47]. My thesis is that this same situation is reversed in the case of the Witness-awareness. The Witness, who has focused the consciousness through meditative practice and made the unconscious layers diaphanous, is accessing the same *magic* (or archetypal) fields of knowledge as the magic consciousness. However, unlike the magic consciousness the Witness does not import the meaning from outside events (and is not bound to concrete objects), but witnesses the emergence or presence of the same meaning, in which subject and object are enveloped, within him or herself. This is indeed comparable to lucid dreaming. Because the Witness masters and is conscious of the deeper layers of the psyche, he or she can apprehend the world as self-sense or self-felt in what equals a full-blown ESP. Hence, the "paradoxical flowing into each other" of the intra-personal and the inter-personal layers can in light of the synchronicity-theory more correctly be conceptualized as *coincidence* of the intra-personal and the inter-personal layers. Furthermore, this coincidence is not 'reached' but always already present. The only thing that is reached is the awareness of it. In this line also Lao Tzu:

47 The physical modality of these fields is what Rupert Sheldrake with his theory of the morphogenetic fields and Ervin Laszlo with his Akasha-field speculate about.

Without going outside, you may know the whole world. Without looking through the window, you may see the ways of heaven. The farther you go, the less you know (Lao Tzu, Tao Te King)[48]

The crucial difference between magic consciousness and Witness-awareness is that the Witness is not personally involved in the witnessed unfolding of the coincident microcosmic and macrocosmic play, which for the Witness is but one – the famous, trans-rational (and pre-rational) all-one. Magic consciousness is completely immersed in the for it egocentric unconscious coincidence between inside and outside, dream and waking reality, to a degree that it is sure to die if it for instance does not literally act out in waking life what it has seen in a dream[49]. In a sense this is also correct for the magic consciousness, because not acting out the dream would interrupt the emotional identification and 'vital connex,' which practically is vital for attraction and killing of game, and logically for its psychic consistence – just as the ego dies when its illusory character is unveiled in the meeting with the self. The Witness on the other hand, who through the observation and witnessing without acting or re-acting (as Jung did) has detached him or herself from the observed and witnessed, is completely autonomous in relation to the witnessed. If I assume correctly that the oneness of observer and observed is a synchronistic reflection, then the personality and perspective of the Witness has dissolved in the synchronistic coincidence of micro- and macrocosm, while for the Witness there is no synchronistic reflection since this again would presuppose a reflecting mind constitutive for an ego-personality. The Witness has transcended the profane condition and conditioning – ready to consciously enter the trans-archaic epicenter. This state of the Witness is commonly understood to be free and at peace, because it is unaffected by the energetic play of active life. There is another reason, though, for the Witness to actually experience peace in all its variations. As earlier described, the Witness can only detach from emotions, urges and drives by making them conscious and 'letting them go.' This calms emotions, urges and drives, through letting them fade into nothing intra-personally and inter-personally by not forming part of escalatory, mutually conflict enhancing dynamics. However, due to the lawful (symbolical) coincidence of micro- and macrocosm, the inner calm and balance of the Witness also forces a macrocosmic, synchronistic correspondence. Through mastering the self, the yogi masters the universe. These trans-personal effects, this trans-personal 'power', however, manifests locally and not globally, grounded in the Witness. The Yogi/Witness, who as bodily microcosm still as well exist in time and space and thus still as well is a local phenomenon, does not force his or her local condition on the global condition, establishing peace on

48 Quoted after www.Taoism.net and *Tao Te Ching: Annotated & Explained*, published by SkyLight Paths in 2006.

49 Cf. Levy-Bruhl 1978, 100-102.

earth valid for everyone. The Witness much more forces the global to give a local, synchronistic reflection centering on the Witness – which of course also influences the local surrounding and from there can spread in the common, causal (or chaotic) rings.

This then explains the trans-rational work of the Taoist rainmaker. It was not enough for the rainmaker to come from a country in Tao, as he himself suggests. It was only through proving that he was a true master of his self, by calming and harmonizing his self against the odds of disharmonious and unbalanced surroundings – so that the synchronistic reflection and compensatory need in form of rain had to fall.

4. Consequences for Transrational Peace Studies

Before concluding this thesis, I will in this chapter sketch out some of the consequences of my research and analysis for a transrational oriented peace philosophy and practice. These consequences concern those two areas, which as always are inseparably connected; ontological and anthropological assumptions about the world we live in – and the thereby deriving implications for a possible peace-philosophy and practice. This sketch is relatively easily drawn, since even though the concept of synchronicity is a new introduction into the debate, it does after all not contribute with substantially new insights regarding ontology and anthropology. Mostly, it simply underscores established concepts, offers an alternative perspective on other known phenomena and again radicalizes third concepts. How this exactly is, will be the subject of the first sub-chapter.

In regard to practice, there are some interesting new possibilities, but due to above reason also here my research mainly underscores established outlines. Due to the radicalization which the principle of correspondence is subjected to through the synchronicity theory, this principle can according to my research be applied correspondingly more radically – to the degree that even divinatory methods might be applicable in certain circumstances (which is on the magic and mythic level of peace work). However, the potentially most interesting contribution of my research to the field of peace studies, I find in the import of consciousness-structures or frames of reference into the diagram of Transrational Peace. Through the altered or widened understanding of projections and their at times underlying circumstances, and the fundamental validation of many pre-modern assertions, which the acceptance of synchronicity leads to, many conflicts which basically root in different cognitive ways of understanding the world can now be approached in a renewed fashion, and with different suppositions. An example in this direction shall be provided. First, however, I shall briefly take up the thread at the coincidence of self and world, archaic and non-dual.

4.1. The Suspension of the Contact Border

The argued synchronistic coincidence of self and world has in my earlier above outline its correlation in the coincidence of what I termed the archaic and the non-dual consciousness structure – or rather, the Witnesses' conscious access of the archaic structure. As argued, the archaic structure corresponds to the episode on the contact border, in other words to the material, physical surface of life, and in terms of life and peace with physical survival and coverage of basic needs such as sleep, nutrition, and excretion. Meanwhile, the archaic was also described as the original, unconscious "being in the reality of oneness" (Neumann), the structure where the human (un)consciousness is in identity with the universe. To show that this archaic identity not is a pathological, psychological fallacy due to undeveloped cognitive potential, but has to be understood as literal identity, to show that the archaic is where the true magic happens, has been one aim of this paper. To experience ESP phenomena, pre-cognitive dreams – in the end what normally is called intuition and what Merriam Webster defines as "a natural ability or power that makes it possible to know something without proof or evidence: a feeling that guides a person to act a certain way without fully understanding why"[50]- is only possible if there in the human operates a form of mind which has universal, space and time transcending access to information, and at the same time is capable of making sense of this information. Probably everyone who has been in a survival situation and has experienced how time slows down, how the body suddenly takes over and simply knows what to do, and proves to be capable of unimaginable things, has had an experiences of this immediate knowledge in the archaic state. Accounts of near-death experiences and the 'peace of the trench' are a whole chapter on its own, which underpin these thoughts. This universal mind is what Jung called the self and found to be the central unifying phenomena in the deepest layer of the psyche – and which mythic logic in its beginning ego-awareness experiences as exterior phenomena. The last thing people think about and experience in these archaic survival situations, albeit it has everything to do with it, is the physical contact border. In a sense, it is suspended. These situations when the body takes over and simply 'knows' how to move and flows as one with the surroundings are truly amazing. I have myself experienced a situation where I with a three metric ton heavy double-sized, fast running forklift truck ran through a closing gate with a speed of 30 mph in a way which tore in parts the gate and the seat I was sitting on, without a scratch on myself. The bystanders watching the scene could not believe how nothing had happened to me, while one of the bystanders was sure there must have been angels watching

[50] http://www.merriam-webster.com/dictionary/intuition. Accessed 30.04.2015.

over me. It is exactly extra-ordinary situations like this, which also nowadays turn people to look for acausal reasons and explanations. In a way the angel-theory is not so far off the mark. When I understand angels as symbols or allegories for those archetypal fields, which the synchronicity-concept implies, and those fields furthermore are ordered by the central, unifying archetype, this universal mind which as exterior phenomena among other has been called God and in its interior reflection the self, and these archetypal manifestations rise here and now in a continuous creation as dynamic interplay of instinct and spirit (or matter and mind) from what Jung called the *Unus Mundus*, the psychoid, undifferentiated primal chaos - and extreme-situations as the just described are characterized by the waking consciousness being relegated to a bystander position where it can *witness* instinct and spirit taking over and working as one – then is not only the contact border suspended, but in a sense one can also speak about angels and divine intervention. Crucial to note is that it is in the contact border of the episode that both matter and spirit manifest and suspend each other – and not in some far off phantasy-realm (albeit thoughts and phantasies as well leave their imprints in the world).

I am not advocating to uncontrollably throwing oneself into life-threatening situations in order to experience the self. More advisable is surely the meditative, yogic way, which aims at the same goal without all the adrenaline. However, many traditional yoga practices in many ways seem to resemble an art of controlled near-death experiences. The extreme fasting practiced as initiation to enter various order of *sannyasins,* but for instance also the practice of *prãnãyãma,* which ideally aims at nothing short of complete stopping of the breath and evidently allows some yogis to enter into cataleptic stasis where both heart-rhythm and breath is slowed down to a degree which otherwise only is witnessed shortly before certain death, points clearly in this direction (Cf. Eliade 1977, 65). A telling test of some yogis' ability consists thus also in being buried alive for periods of up to ten days, without taking harm (Ibid.). That the yogi through such psychophysical exercises searches to control and master his or her consciousness and physiological processes to a degree which enables him or her to enter the archaic, non-dual state, but conscious and free, is no new idea and for instance also shared by Eliade (Ibid. 54). That this is possible and experienced as the most profound peace makes this a peace-philosophical relevant topic.

4.2. Synchronicity and Peace Philosophy

My main concern here however is not only with the extra-ordinary manifestations of archaic non-duality, and how to experience them. It is especially with these everyday manifestations of ESP and synchronicity, which easily are recognizable for everyone as soon as one knows what to look for. As I have outlined, I together with Jung deduce that they have far reaching onto-, anthropo- and ecological implications. Not only do they, when logically followed to the end, culminate in, and necessitate, some form of non-dual all-oneness. The whole 'interim calculation' is of highest, peace-philosophical interest. When these phenomena are taken as seriously as they deserve, it makes little difference whether they are explained by Rupert Sheldrake´s (1981) theory of morphogenetic fields, Erwin Lazlo´s (2000) Akasha-field, which operates with spacetime transcending information exchange rooting in the holo-field of the quantum-vacuum – or as done here with Jung´s theory of synchronicity and the archetypes. The crucial point is that mind proves to operate outside of the brain as well, includes nature, and not is confined to space and time. This, it seems to me, is already something of the most profound, which can be said about peace, since it has pervasive repercussions on the attitude towards the world we live in. Here I can only rephrase Dietrich, who states that whoever disassociates phenomena of mind from the encompassing systems to which they are imminent, and restricts them to the narrow confines of individuals, subjects or persons, necessarily must experience the surrounding world as mind-less (Dietrich 2008, 376-377). This, then, is the cosmological premise to exploit nature as resource. The attitude would be completely different, if there was an agreement that the *Mitwelt*[51] not only is alive, but also endowed with mind (Ibid.).

The emerging worldview which opens up, fits with, and follows from above analysis and insights, is in my view exactly this 'science of mind' (the German word *Geisteswissenschaft* would be the more fitting term – since it is synonymous with humanities and here in a double sense gains its original meaning back) which Dietrich in reference to Gregory Bateson, Ken Wilber and C. G. Jung has outlined in the first volume of the *"Variationen über die vielen Frieden"* series (2008)[52]. This is of course no wonder, since Dietrich´s outline from the outset already was my frame of reference. However, that my investigation into synchronicity and its consequences in the end still would fit with the transrational theory, was not a given. Therefore I will here 'highlight the

51 This German term which I borrow from Dietrich (2008) contains the double connotation and possible literal translation of 'together-world' and 'middle-world' (My translation). In the latter translation is its root in German mythology visible, where *Mitwelt* probably is connected to *Mittelerde* and denotes the realm and earth, which humans inhabit and lays between, that is in the middle of, heaven and hell – while the latter as well can be understood as the extremes in another frame for possible states of mind. In my use of the term, the emphasis lies on 'together-world', addressing the surrounding world including nature in which humans are embedded and stresses the circumstance that humans are not disconnected from the surrounding world but intrinsically connected with it and life basically is a 'together', where the human and the human mind is not ontologically different from all other phenomena.

52 Hence I refer the reader to this work and here especially the last chapter "Transrationale Friedenswissenschaften" (Dietrich 2008, 319-377).

highlights,' and show how this outline is congruent, and where it diverges from my own findings.

4.2.1. Science of Mind

As outlined, it is in synchronistic phenomena evident that mind as a meaning constructing phenomena also operates and manifests outside of the human psyche and brain. Since Jung understood that conscious manifestations of mind, such as thought, learning, memory and the like, are ordered by unconscious mind-forces which he termed archetypes, he deduced correctly that in light of the synchronistic evidence, these archetypes had to be understood as field-phenomena encompassing the individual mental ego-consciousness. If the same transpersonal fields of mind order individual human minds, this means translated to system-theoretical terminology, that a person is an open system (and only can be termed person with a proper ego when the mental layer is integrated) embedded in at least one wider system with a corresponding mind. This would be the unsubtle 'monotheistic' result, where this universal mind would correspond to God. Dietrich remarks again and again, and in my view correctly, that this would not mean God as ontological Other, outside-standing and from the cosmos a separated God, but as an archetypal peak of consciousness (Dietrich 2008, 372). God is then the all-embedding system – the all-one. Meanwhile, when mind can not only be ascribed to individual organisms, but also to greater social and ecological systems, it would follow that groups of people, societies and cultures as well have a collective mind, and a collective consciousness with the corresponding unconsciousness (in agreement with this Dietrich 2008, 373).

This form of holism is no new concept, and also Dietrich is aware of the critiques and problems of such a suggestion. Totalitarianism and fascism are equally holistic concepts, where the civil rights and liberties of the individual are undermined in the name of the greater good and whole (Ibid.). I agree with Dietrich that this indeed becomes a danger when the collective mind is ascribed to abstract categories such as nation, homeland, home and the like (Ibid.). Dietrich means that these abstracts much more are expressions of the pathological ego of these collectives' minds[53] (Ibid.). The German Federal

[53] It has to be noted that Dietrich uses the term ego differently than I do. What I term ego Dietrich terms 'I', whereas what Dietrich means with ego much more corresponds to what Jung called the shadow. While the shadow for Jung represented unconscious, rejected parts of the personality, the ego in Dietrich's sense means really an egoistic frame of reference characterized by egoistical wants and striving, which likewise root in an unconsciousness and thus unbalanced activation of the archaic, magic and mythic layers. The egocentrism of the magic and mythic structure is traditionally no problem in the historically corresponding societies, where intra and

Republic would then correspond to the German collective mind as the Jungian shadow corresponds to the ego. Accepting mind as systemic feature and the consequential concept of minds embedded in minds means thus not to accept totalitarianism, but to accept that these collective minds are subject to the same psychological dynamics as the individual mind – and hence can show the same pathological symptoms as an individual mind.

> A not by egocentrism sickened system consists of concrete relations between equals and towards the higher-level system, while these relations mostly are cooperative, sometimes conflictive but principally not competing, as social Darwinism assumes. Especially are its borders transparent, permeable, never exclusive. There exist social coherencies such as families, neighborhoods, village societies, work groups and the like, which also are equipped with a collective mind. Individuals, however, belong simultaneously to several systems. They can switch between those but latest at the higher-level systems are all those contemporary adopted borders again transformed. Something like a tribe, a state, a people or a nation is always an assumption, a construct, an imagination of temporal, spatial and personnel limited reach, which in the systemic approach never legitimizes to any exclusion or rivalry (Dietrich 2008, 374. My translation).

These are obviously important points stressed by Dietrich. Since humans are part of these 'mindful' relations, are guided by them and simultaneously form them as well, I can with the system concept of feedback-loops settle the decade old dispute of whether the human is the root of its synchronicities or completely subject to the wider minds, by stating that it both is subject and initiator. Meanwhile, not only would it from the individual's ego-perspective be regressive, limiting and strategically unreasonable to identify with and adhere to just one and only temporary existing sub-system. The only reasonable point of orientation is always the higher-level system, which in the final analysis is the very system, which comprises all the other systems and is the only closed system – and what transrational terminology calls the all-one. Relevant is the consideration that when the self of the personal mind in the end is coincident with the all-one, then the self of those collective minds is as well coincident with the all-one. This can also be no other way, since every existence is a temporary '*exsisto*' in the sense of 'stepping out of' the all-one. Humans, and everything else, are not 'thrown' into the cosmos but emerge from it, bound to dissolve back into it. Since no energy is lost in a closed system, it should be safe to say that this dynamic play of life is eternal. The question of peace is in this perspective the question of the composition and harmonious flow of energy in the dynamic emergence and dissolution of oscillating, meaningful systems within systems.

---

inter-systemic compulsions, or rather the consciousness of the collective mind, balances the individual unconsciousness and ego-centrism and kept it at bay.

4.2.2. Universal Peace and Practice

If there is a universal system, there must consequently also exist something like a universal peace. In a sense 'true' peace is just imaginable from this universal a-perspective. The violent death of the fish I ate was surely not a peaceful act from the perspective of the fish, while the fish helped to keep my system in harmonious flow and at peace. The death of the ascetic who dies from starvation, because he refuses to kill another organism, is surely also a violent act – which maybe, does not let his mind dissolve directly into the peace of the all-one - which is the only system that does not gets eaten. The question of peace becomes a question of perspective, and thus transferred into a plurality. There exist as many small peaces as perspectives, systems and reality planes – and as many manifestations of the universal peace. Besides this, there is one more characteristic of the all-one and its countless sub-systems, which is crucial in regard to peace practice. Since the all-one is not a fixed entity, because life is not a static structure, but in constant flux, emerging in ever changing manifestations and meaning-constellations, there cannot be one fixed state of peace. The rule is what I already cited at the beginning of the second chapter; peaces are a dynamic equilibrium. This means that there is no peace 'attainable,' since it would be flux gone the next moment, there is no one-size-fits-all, not one solution transferable to another. Context and circumstances are ever changing and with them the answer to what a dynamic equilibrium is or needs in the moment and in the long run. Mechanistic peace intervention becomes virtually impossible in front of the complexity, subtlety and sublimity of life and mind – and reckless in its belief to be able to fix anything for the better. Luckily enough, living systems are self-regulating, and greater minds than the human mind are at work as well in keeping the balance. Still, when the deeper forces of the greater mind sends its compensatory impulses, the sheer existence of peace-studies and peace-workers can indeed be understood as systemic 'message' that something is out of balance – while peace-work otherwise is one of these paradoxical jobs where the worker makes herself redundant when the work is done well. In this sense, I will in the following mention what my particular contribution in regard to consciousness-layers and synchronicity means and can contribute with to the more practical aspect of peace-work, as far as this has not already happened.

4.3. Working with Magic

The first point I shall mention concerns the use of divinatory methods for determining a fruitful course of action in accordance with the harmony of the wider system. Since Jung´s synchronicity-hypothesis originated in an attempt to explain the stunningly intelligent answers gained by consulting the I Ging, it follows that as far as the synchronicity-hypothesis is considered coherent and applicable; a theoretical justification for the application of the I Ging is given as well. As banal as the experiment might seem, according to the synchronicity-theory the experimenter would indeed function as channel for the all-one, which synchronistically manifests as the gained hexagram and whose meaning is encoded in the language of the I Ging. From the outset, and since I have associated synchronicity with magic and mythic manifestations and logics, I would only recommend its use in this context. This means as far as family or community matters are at stake or the own person in relation to the family or the community. On a second thought, however, and as far as heads of state function as temporal Father or Mother of the Nation, and their personal synchronicities reflect the state of the collective mind of the collective they represent, experiments in this direction would be interesting. This would furthermore be in accord with more traditional understandings of these matters, where often the dreams of the chief were considered those relevant for the whole tribe (Cf. Levy-Bruhl 1923, 97).

The second point I shall only mention here without further exploration but where the here explored consciousness layers might be applicable, concerns those conflicts, which seem unsolvable by discursive means due to mutually excluding worldviews. As paradigmatic example I can take the Yup'ik eskimos, who make their home on the coastal environment of Nelson Island. One characteristic of this traditional hunting society is that they view animals as nonhuman persons, which whom they through hunting enter into very personal relationships with (Cf. Fienup-Riordan 1994, 167-168). When a young man kills his first seal, first of all this seal is understood to have offered itself to enter into a relationship with the young man, and secondly the killing and appropriate handling of its body means that the seal will be reborn and again appear in front of the same young man, ready to enter a new cycle of death and rebirth (Ibid. 169-170). A rejected kill or inability to kill the seal on part of the man will be taken as offense on part of the seal, which will result in that the seal will not appear again (Ibid.). Practically, this means that game is understood as an infinite resource, as long as every animal that shows up is killed. Now, when the Canadian government shows up and states that the Yup'ik have to limit their fishing and hunting, because the animals otherwise will be extinct, this is diametrically opposite to the understanding of those people – and negotiations and talks between western governments and Inuit societies have accordingly proved extremely difficult due to a lack of mutual understanding. It seems to me that the contemporary practice in such cases increasingly involves to actually give special rights to those communities, due to the injustices and violence they historically and still face from Western cultural domination. This is of course better than nothing. However, there seems to be little to no understanding for the validity and reality of the emic perspective of the Yup'ik on side of the Western government. While I do not doubt the mathematical calculations concerning fish populations, and the threat of extinction due to massive overfishing on side of modern society, I miss an academic understanding for the reality of soul-connections in the magic layer, an understanding of what the Aboriginal dream-time could be apart from a good story. In this direction, I believe further investigations into synchronicity and likewise phenomena might prove fruitful, and might lead to conflict transformations built on mutual understanding, where the Yup´ik are allowed to fish, not out of guilt by simultaneous and continuous misunderstanding, but due to an appraisal of the validity of their point of view.

4.3.1. Consciousness and the Art of Peace

In many ways I can subscribe to the preamble of the UNESCO Constitution, which states, "since wars begin in the minds of men, it is in the minds of men that the defenses of peace must be constructed."[54] It contains the fruitful focus on the phenomena of mind – and even though the unnecessary martial sounding 'defenses of peace,' which are believed having to be constructed in the seemingly dangerous minds of men and thereby makes the mind to the enemy of peace (albeit a mindless peace seems exactly that - mindless, unattractive and the question where exactly this peace should be experienced if not in and through the mind is pressing), it also might somehow imply the beautiful idea of peace being the natural way of things, uninterrupted by the intervention of man[55]. I will here stick to the focus on mind, since both wars and peaces begin, end, and are experienced in the mind.

As implied above, the ideal of a perfect peace with a conflict-free world must remain an inhuman utopia, since life not is static, the human condition implies digesting life and eventually being digested, and conflicts in themselves are nothing but the expression and perspectival experienced energy in transformation of a life in flux. What can be done is to transform the (personal and collective) perspective, and stop to form part of unnecessary, mutually conflict-enhancing dynamics rooting in egocentric ignorance and adherence. As already pointed out, and in line with the topics of this paper I understand most, if not virtually all preventable and transformable conflicts, to be rooted in egocentric ignorance and adherence; which always also implies inactivated consciousness potential. In this perspective peace work reveals itself as the facilitation of consciousness rising. How this process of consciousness-development normally occurs naturally in the ontogenesis and presumably has

---

54 http://www.unesco.org/new/en/unesco/about-us/who-we-are/history/constitution/ Accessed 01.05.2015.

55 Whether this interpretation of peace being the natural way of things also is intended by the Originator of the preamble, I do not know.

manifested in its collective correlation in history up to the mental layer, has been the topic of the first chapter.

At this point and in relation to the in this paper not discussed power-relations, I thus just want to point out that what from a mental, integrated ego-awareness easily is recognizable as the at times astonishing egocentric cruelty and violent tendency of small children, indeed has its correlative in the correlating collective organizations. Of course, just as every child is different, so is every family-clan, tribe or other collective conglomerate, which I here allege of likewise tendencies. Nevertheless, the logic of blood feud, headhunting, war-raids and constant being at war with the neighbor tribes as for instance characteristic for the tribes on New Guinea, speak a language of its own, and put to shame much of the Romantics wish of joining former times' closeness to nature – as far as this is imagined as a conflict-free and non-violent condition. The sporadic cruelty and egoistical violence of small children is normally no problem for the wider system in which the child is embedded, due to the child´s comparable little amount of power, and only becomes a problem for the wider society later on, if these tendencies are not transcended and integrated in a deeper intra-personal and wider social and inter-personal awareness. Likewise, what from a rational ego-perspective looks like cruel and violent behavior in archaic, magic and mythic societies, I assume to be a relatively small problem from within the logic of those societies, as well as for the wider systems in which they are embedded, due to their comparable little amount of power. On the other hand, when an organization such as the United States of America, which builds on abstract formal operational principles and for the maintenance of its self-justification presupposes the actual application of its ethical principles, suddenly applies torture, then this constitutes a form of primitivism and incoherence which is hard to find among so-called primitive societies, and constitutes a real problem for the wider system due to its power in relation to the wider system, which obliges to a form of responsibility which this form of egocentric logic cannot fulfill.

I should again note that I not at all understand magic and mythic societies to dwell in a child-like state of consciousness. Much on the contrary, I assume that many of the members of such societies develop their mind and spiritual potential to a much greater degree than contemporary moderns, due to the relation between the archaic and the non-dual and the living-conditions they are embedded in, which in a compensatory manner furthers this form of development. What I assume is a correlation between basic social organization and basic consciousness layers. Just as the child at a state where it just has the mother as reference dwells in archaic fusion, I assume that every modern cosmopolitan, who suddenly would find him or herself on a very small island with just one other person, quickly would enter a state of either archaic fusion or complete separation. Just as ESP and synchronicity is quite common among family members, would the focus on and activation of this plane of reality increase, when the respective family lives separated from wider society. What would be a development of this person towards the archaic or this family towards the magic and mythic within a lifetime in this ontogenetic example has to be understood as blossomed and differentiated collective equivalent in the collective mind-structures and societies, which thus have nothing to do with an evolutionary development process, but much more with circumstances and placement within a potential range of possibilities.

What this little excursion into my first chapter means, is that intra-personal archaic, magic or mythic egocentrism is no problem in a peace perspective, as long as these intra-personal activated layers are balanced by the according inter-personal awareness. The Jungian variant of internal mythic egocentrism is no problem, but coherent and integrated when it through the external recognition of synchronicity lets itself be guided by the self. Likewise is the mental dualism and consequent internal emancipation from the unconscious self no problem when it is balanced by the application of accordingly abstract, ethical principles, in inter-personal relationships. The problems and conflicts (and wars in the collective equivalent) arise as soon as there comes imbalance in the layers between the intra- and inter-personal correspondences. For instance, when the intra-personal archaic body loses its inter-personal basic trust of being secure in the universe (archaic identity between self and universe), fear or insecurity is the result, which on this level is searched compensated by greed, and distorts the whole person (or collectives) towards egoistical striving and the karmic chain of action and reaction is going. Since the processes in the archaic, magic and mythic layer normally proceed unconsciously, and in case of imbalances only find their manifestation in conflictive episodes on the contact border – the best defense of peace consists accordingly in the conscious awareness and witnessing of intra- and inter-personal manifestations. Consciousness, both collective as in the latin root of *conscientia,*meaning 'knowing together' as in the German version *Bewusst-sein,* meaning 'being aware,' reveals itself as a key towards the many peaces.

5. Conclusion

I have begun this work with the hypothesis that there exist a relation between the concepts of synchronicity and the all-one – or that a fruitful relationship between those two theoretical formulations could be established. This would implicit be of highest peace-philosophical interest, because the all-one, and consequently any inquiry into the nature of the all-one, is of highest peace-philosophical interest. This is so, since the all-one as theoretical formulation describes the relation and interdependence of everything with everything else, from which the ethics of peace derive. It validates a call for holistic orientation instead of egoistical striving and makes the orientation towards the many peaces a reasonable and worthwhile enterprise. Based on this assumption, I asked how synchronicity relates to the transpersonality of the all-one – and how it consequently can be understood in a transrational perspective. A special sub-question in this regard I searched to answer was in how far the oneness of observer and observed in the Witness-awareness can be described as synchronistic relation. In other words, can the paradoxical flowing into each other of the intra-personal and inter-personal layers in the dissolution of the perspective be described as a synchronistic phenomenon? What I wanted to find out was thus whether synchronicity could be described as the medium through which transpersonality and finally the all-one manifests itself for the observer, which in turn would mean that a regard for synchronicity would be an everyday mean and entrance to the all-one as living reality.

My original hypothesis regarding the relation between synchronicity and the all-one I have by and large found confirmed. That is because there not only exist a certain historical connection in the development of those two concepts as they present themselves today, since Jung developed his synchronicity-concept in close collaboration with Wolfgang Pauli, who was one of the founding fathers of quantum mechanics, and the inseparability of observer and observed, hitherto one of the best established arguments resulting in a concrete all-one, directly results from translating the findings of quantum mechanics. However, the from my perspective far more interesting, fruitful and possible connection emerged when I integrated the Jungian synchronicity theory with the transrational, systemic science of mind as outlined by Dietrich (2008). In my interpretation of Dietrich´s holistic and systemic perspective, the all-one presents itself as the all-encompassing system which can be called existence, universe or cosmos but is more than the sum of its parts in that it has, or rather is, a mind and as thus also can be termed God, World-Soul or Brahman (Cf. Dietrich 2008, 394). The countless sub-systems emerging out of the all-one, from galaxies to molecules and everything in between from plants, animals, humans, societies, eco-systems, planets to planetary systems are then equally equipped with mind – or at the very least equally carriers of information exchange within the larger mind. In a holistic logic this means that the sub-systems do not determine the larger system - and systemic logic adds that the sub-systems neither are completely determined by the larger system(s) but through series of feedback-loops stands in a creative interrelationship with the wider system(s), which thus all the time is in a dynamic flux. Hence, humans are describable as focal points in time and space experiencing, reflecting and transforming collective energy. Humans are thus neither powerless nor are they omnipotent. They have partial power, all the time balancing between self-preservation and self-transgression. That this is a valid, empirically founded postulate is in my thesis underscored by the synchronicity-theory, which describes the coincidence of intra-personal phenomena of mind and external phenomena, or the simultaneous coincidence of the same psychic content in separate individuals and the like, in an acausal manner. These empirical, albeit only limited statistically reproducible, observations termed synchronicity suggest that many phenomena of mind have to be understood as collective field-phenomena, operating as well prior to time and space but still consistent with the postulate of mind as systemic feature of system within systems. This does meanwhile not interfere with the contemporary conventional understanding of knowledge being transferred causally via lectures, books and other physical means in space and time as well.

These considerations and findings have obviously tremendous implications for the human attitude towards the *mitwelt* because they in the here presented interpretation argue that human and the human mind neither is ontologically different from all other phenomena nor separable from them in the first place. A certain anthropomorphism seems justified and at its place. A logically coherent consequence would for instance be to make no difference in how one treats humans and animals but meet everyone with the same respect and reverence. This does of course not mean that I expect to have intellectual conversations about Sloterdijk´s latest book with my dog – but then again do I neither expect to have those with most humans. It means that it would be incoherent to entertain intensive livestock farming if one would not treat humans the same way[56]. Regarding the question whether one would treat other humans this way, the ethical answer lies in answering the question whether one would like to be subjected oneself to the same treatment. Since their cannot be a fixed rule and final answer in a world where the only constant is change, I am not postulating

[56] This does not imply that I am a proponent of cannibalism. While the explanations of some people practicing cannibalism indeed can be ethically sound and reasonable (See for instance Beth Conklin (2001)), I tend towards the vegetarian alternative as far as possible. The whole complex of practices and implications of killing game in traditional small-scale hunting societies is a topic on its own, which to explore as further investigation in the here presented context would be interesting.

moral rules but pointing to the logical consequences of these circumstances, which in this particular case are questions which everyone has to answer for him or herself all the time again and again.

In the here presented worldview, every system has necessarily its own relative dynamic equilibrium and truth, for which reason there are many small peaces and truths. In a holistic perspective of systems within systems, the 'truths' and 'peaces' of the encompassing systems are arguably on a first glance as well more encompassing and greater until the 'universal' truth of the all-one – along which to orientate I have presented as the most reasonable and ethical. A hypothetical written testimony of the all-one, or a sub-system still large enough to go as a god, (as the Bible and Koran claim to constitute) might in my view theoretically hold a certain validity and coherence over time, just as most people are capable of making agreements with themselves or others over time and fulfill their self-made promises. However, such agreements and static testimonies would be poor and unfulfilling substitutes for a personal and immediate dialog and intimate relationship with the all-one – a relationship, which in my view necessarily always already exists in the fact of existence and leads me to the further implications of the synchronicity theory.

When the individual mind is embedded in wider minds, to a certain degree determined by those and as well stands in a relationship of feedback-loops with these, one would suspect that there at times would be coincidences in these mind-contents. This is of course to a large degree always the case and causally explainable, when for instance individual attitudes, thoughts, concerns and the like are explainable by the public discourses or sub-discourses existing in the wider society in which the individual is embedded and forms part of. However, one would also suspect simultaneous, from the individual perspective not causally explainable coincidences. Just as my sweat pore might understand that its impulse to sweat comes from neurotransmitters innervated by the sympathetic nerve system but not understands why (or just how) this meaningfully relates to the heightened heartbeat, the widened pupils and the fearful pictures in the brain – because it does not see the tiger in front of the larger system of which it forms part. Analogue sorts of meaningful, often synchronous coincidences between different minds, which are not causally explainable from the personal perspective I have argued do happen and are what Jung termed synchronicity. While my just posed example suggests that these connections after all could have a causal explanation, which to investigate further along these lines would be an interesting and I believe worthwhile endeavor[57], I followed in this work Jung´s in

[57] By this I mean to investigate synchronistic occurrence in larger systems with relevance for larger systems. That could be the phenomena of important scientific investigations made at different ends of the world simultaneously without causal connection, as for instance the independent discovery of infinitesimal calculus of Leibniz and Newton, the simultaneous but independent formulation of evolution theory by Charles Darwin and Wallace in 1858, the integral theory of Aurobindo and Gebser but also stunning coincidences as Hernán Cortés bloody conquest of the

every sense personal perspective on synchronicity[58]. Jung investigated and came to the result of an in his view occasional and meaningful coincidence of the personal and a universal mind from the other end of the range, so to say. He did not start at an all-one and from there worked his way down to the individual mind but started at the depths of the individual mind and followed how the depth of the psyche manifests in dreams, emotions and phantasies and eventually on the visible contact border of the episode in a symbolic albeit still causally way, sometimes as neurotic, sometimes as what is considered normal behavior. During (and due to) his study of the symbolic manifestations emerging from the depth of the psyche he was able to recognize synchronistic coincidences, that is 'acausal' symbolical correspondences, between the content at the depth of the psyche and manifestations in the visible *Mitwelt.* Since deep psychic content normally is unconscious and the incidences where deep psychic content becomes conscious and personally visible are rather rare, as in an affect or ecstasy, the corresponding strong and clear synchronicities are accordingly rare, which is why Jung publicly postulated the emergence of synchronicity as occasional phenomena happening in connection with the constellation of an archetype – that is deep psychic content breaking into and possessing consciousness. However, since deep psychic content, the Jungian archetypes, always also exist albeit unconscious, it is only consequential to assume that the synchronistic correspondence also always exists, albeit invisible. That means that the visible world would be symbolically and immediately corresponding to the personal psyche – and every unusual event in the surroundings has its correlative within the psyche, which however is invisible for the ego-consciousness because this ego normally after all not is that conscious (hence the unconscious) and in sync with its self. That Jung privately came to the same conclusion is affirmed by Jung´s practice of all the time watching for synchronicities as in unusual events in the surroundings and deducing conclusions from these outer manifestations for the intra-psychic condition. Further affirmative in this direction is Jung´s theory of the psychoid archetype-as-such. Translated to transrational peace-philosophy and practice, this would imply a radicalized applicability of the principle of correspondence as outlined by Dietrich (2015), where not only inter-personal patterns build over time would correspond to the corresponding intra-personal layers equally build over time but also could be correlated in a more

Aztec empire at a time where Montezuma II due to mythic revelations expected the epiphany of Quetzalcoatl, a god normally depicted as winged serpent – but also as fair-skinned bearded man, reminiscent of the Spanish Conquistadores.

58 As mentioned earlier do I understand Jung´s fixation on 'acausality' as rooting in his almost obsessive occupation with opposites and their integration, which for me among much other points to a complex in the sexual layer of Jung´s psyche.

immediate fashion – as practiced by Jung[59]. Further research, discussions and outlines in this direction would be an interesting perspective and entrance to bring forth the research into synchronicity. My concern in this work, however, went into a different direction.

At this point my outline of the diagram of Transrational Peace, where the first four layers correspond to Jung´s conceptualization of the intra-psychic person, becomes relevant. The psychoid archetype-as-such is Jung´s term for the yet undifferentiated, diffuse oneness of instinct and archetype while the latter two terms correlate to matter and mind/spirit, in that Jung saw instincts as physiologically based chemical reactions in the body (in further consequence the 'building blocks' of matter), while the archetypes describe the unconscious foundation of mind activity which makes sense of matter and since Descartes has been viewed as ontologically different from matter. This Cartesian dualism, which was an hopeless albeit far-reaching attempt to save God as ontological other, is in Jung´s formulation of the archetype-as-such suspended, in that it grounds both mind and matter in the same oneness. For this reason Christian religious dogmatist scream up and not only Buber but also Wilber, who at times as well want to understand spirit as ontological different from matter, criticized Jung (Wilber 2000, 345). Meanwhile, the archetype-as-such corresponds in my outline to the archaic level, Dietrich´s epicenter and Gebser´s archaic undifferentiated oneness of consciousness with the world. More exactly, it corresponds to matter viewed on the quantum level, to the undifferentiated probability-fields, where observer and observed cannot be differentiated but coincide in a diffuse oneness. It is first in the process of 'zooming out' that apparently more or less predictable particles and later atoms, chemicals, molecules and in this case eventually the human body and the visible world appears. Now something interesting happens; by again 'zooming in' in the different direction[60], that is out in the cosmos, planets, solar systems and galaxies appear and if it were technically possible eventually the outer edge of the universe, which is the continuous process of creation, the Big Bang, where the all-one as closed system closes and whose modality I believe is reasonable to assume equal with the modality of matter on the quantum level. This anyway is what I believe Jung meant with the archetype-as-such being the microcosmic equivalent to the primal chaos in the macrocosm and if I am correct, then there is a synchronistic coincidence between the outer edge of the universe and the undifferentiated modality of the matter on the quantum level I am made of. Here

[59] And in different variations probably by the greater part of outstanding intelligent individuals and people throughout history of mankind, of which I just have mentioned Leibniz, Schopenhauer, Agrippa von Nettesheim, Paracelsus, Albertus Magnus and traditional Chinese philosophy, albeit this list could be continued.

[60] One could also imagine this as continuous 'zooming out', which would change the perspective but not alter the finding.

I have set the frame for an *energetic* worldview where micro- and macrocosm coincide. An equal process of 'zooming out' did I in line with Jung describe for the differentiation of consciousness. In the magic layer the archetype-as-such differentiates into the complementary pair of instinct and archetypal image and can in terms of consciousness be described as 'point-like unity' between instinct and image – inner emotion and outer experience - an unity quite real in this realm and from a mental perspective describable as synchronicity. This level correlates to the sexual layer, which as principle in a sense seeks the unification of the just differentiated complementary pair, creates families and as energy is highly creative and close to the original creation of the archaic. This differentiation continues via polar enclosedness in the mythic until the apparent dualistic nature of ego-consciousness in the mental layer, where the psychological *persona* is complete and potentially capable of consciously acting in the episode – corresponding to the visible world of everyday experience. From an anthropocentric perspective, mythological descriptions of humans inhabiting the middle-world gain renewed credibility, when humans (and every other entity in the for humans visible world) inhabits this middle-kingdom between the inner chaos of the atoms and the chaos at the outer edge of the cosmos.

However, as argued and outlined is the ego in many ways nothing more than a narrative fiction, a mental abstraction which in its only apparent individuality corresponds to the likewise only apparent individuality of the body as visible in everyday life, which likewise is bound to die. Not only in a systemic perspective becomes the interdependence and embeddedness of body and mind with everything else apparent, for which reason the freedom of the by 'enlightened' philosophers postulated autonomous individual in the end was a negotiated compromise between individual wants and social needs – and vice versa. The ego is as much or little master of its fate as the body is of its survival and really quite dependent and subject to larger and deeper forces and circumstances guiding its fate. The only possibly free and autonomous being is the all-one. What Jung thus identified as the intra-personal ordering and guiding principle of the whole person including the ego and consequently termed the self, can in a holistic and systemic perspective anyway not be anything else than the all-one, when the whole determines the parts. That the most personal literally is the most universal that atman and Brahman are one that self, god and world coincide is underpinned by the synchronicity-theory. This conclusion, which I reached by arguably rational arguments, can according to transpersonal psychology and yoga-philosophy be experienced when the Witness-awareness enters the non-dual epicenter. Consciousness is in the here developed perspective then a continuum, symbolically reaching from the archaic roots in undifferentiated quantum-fields to the likewise undifferentiated outer edges of the universe where being turns into not-being. For peace-philosophy this is of highest relevance, because the two epicenter of the diagram of Transrational Peace show to synchronistically coincide all the time everywhere. Consequently, the ethical imperative of treating other as one would treat oneself turns into a literal reality; treating the other really means to treat one's self, to treat the holy (in the sense of "wholly") all-one. Jesus word, "truly I tell you, whatever you did for one of the least of these brothers and sisters, you did for me" (Matthew 25, 40), turns here into a comprehensible, transrational truth. More important in the service of peace on the contact border of the episode, I do not have to say.

While the above just stated could perform as peroration, in the spirit of Innsbruckian Peace Studies and Jungian psychology I will end this thesis on a personal note and thus close the circle when connecting to the introductory personal perspective. I believe to have delivered a more or less coherent and logical argument for why synchronicity can describe a modality of transpersonality and how the paradoxical flowing into each other of the intra-personal and inter-personal layers in the Witness-awareness can be described as synchronistic occurrence - and how this always already is the case. In relation to Jung's concept of compensation and individuation I further pointed to a way how synchronicity can be used in a personal relationship with the self. However, this description occurred from a mental ego-perspective and only makes sense on this level. For the Witness there is no synchronicity, because there is no differentiation between inside and outside because all there is is the world, just as for the archaic consciousness there is no coincidence of self and world because all there is is the self. "Truth is a pathless land" said Jiddu Krishnamurti[61] and I agree in the sense that I might be able to describe and imagine these states and the self from my ego-perspective but never can write and explain myself or any other into them, because words necessitate a perceiving subject and an objectifying language – exactly what archaic and conscious awareness and the self are not. They simply are. Language is the boon and bane of the middle kingdom, while archaic oneness and Witness awareness dwell at the respective outer edges of this realm or right at the center – depending on the perspective.

Hence, an approach like mine is inherently limited and has to be aware of its limitations. Especially when it comes to topics like synchronicity and the self, the dangers of projection and confusion between ego and self are great and can as argued easily lead to narcissistic inflation or solipsism, which are two variations of the same circumstance – a thorough egocentrism. Just as an egocentric person can learn from its 'mistakes' by becoming conscious of them and integrate this gained knowledge into a wider ego-awareness, the mistake is only relativized in case of appropriate integration. Likewise, a Jungian work with emotions and unconscious content can lead to an awareness of the self – but not at all is every synchronicity, hunch or emotion a manifestation of the self in the strict sense. This is only a valid proposition in the larger picture and in the frame

61 Quoted after Stuckrad 2004, 214.

of a teleological understanding, implying to actually go the whole way. Otherwise, most synchronicities, just as emotions and ideas, will simply be the reflection and construction of the own ego and its egoistical impulses and emotions. Acting and become enchanted by those synchronicities thus really means to be prisoner of the own mind and to chase the own tail. Synchronicity in itself is thus not genuinely spiritual but simply a modality of the world we live in. As pointed out, alone the recognition of synchronicity already entails a certain degree of ego-centrism and self-reference and does in my view therefore not qualify as recommendable reference frame. Just as sticking the nose in the ground and watching the ants and life in the very small for a while can be an enlightening experience, teaching a lot about the world we all form part of, it seems inappropriate and unpractical to remain with the nose stuck in the ground. Likewise, recognizing synchronicity can be an enlightening experience, from which for instance above considerations can derive – however, remaining in the synchronistic perspective seems to me rather unpractical and inappropriate.

Thus and a bit ironically, the result for me of this work has been to stop being enchanted by synchronistic occurrences. In a sense I have gotten closure with this topic. Old habits die hard and I do still recognize synchronicities in my surroundings. However, most of the time, I understand things in their own context and not simultaneously as synchronistically relating to others or myself. Helpful and instructive for me was the work with the diagram of Transrational Peace as different forms of reference frame in relation to ego-development. To realize my own ego-centrism has at times been a very sobering experience. It was not difficult to realize how my personal worldview aligned to something akin to a full-blown mythic reference frame, with the in my case at least according unconscious ego-centricity. As a consequence and when it comes to cognitive processes, I am these days more concerned with the application of my emphatic ability, both in its tactical and compassionate form. This development has been a liberating experience for me, while seeing myself from the outside still can be quite shocking and I understand that my socialization is an ongoing process. The simultaneous cultivation of internal and external observation without analysis I do experience, as much needed tranquilizing and harmonizing break in this ongoing process of self- and world exploration. However, the next step in my 'consciousness-development' I see in developing my sense of ego-consciousness by simultaneous engagement in wider societal issues – before an eventual retreat into the mountain cave.

I am still fascinated by the implications of synchronicity for ontological questions, however this work has demonstrated me how complicated and literally mind transcending these matters are – and that I have little chances to understand these matters on a cognitive level, let alone my limitations in conveying potential insights as written word. In this sense, if I might have conveyed just some of my own sense of how subtle and 'magic' life is, this text has been a success.

List of references

Adler, Gerhard, and Aniela Jaffé, eds. (1975): *C. G. Jung Letters.* 2 vols. Trans. R. F. C. Hull. Princeton, University Press, Princeton.

Atziz, Robert (1990): *C. G. Jung's Psychology of Religion and Synchronicity.* SUNY Series in Transpersonal and Humanistic Psychology. State University of New York Press, Albany.

Barash, David P. and Charles P. Webel (2009): *Peace and Conflict Studies.* SAGE Publications, Los Angeles.

Bardon, Franz (1982): *Der Weg des Wahren Adepten.* Hermann Bauer Verlag, Freiburg im Breisgau.

Barnes, Cary F. (1962): *The Secret of the Golden Flower.* Harcourt, Brace & World, New York.

Bauman, Zygmunt (1988): *Frihed.* Original title "Freedom", published by Hans Reitzel Forlag A/S, 2003, København.

Beecher, Henry K. (1955): "The Powerful Placebo" in *Journal of the American Medical Association* Volume 159, nr 17, pp. 1602 – 1606.

Bloomfield, Robert B.; Caine, Michael P. and Dennis T. Jaffe (1975): *TM: Discovering Inner Energy and Overcoming Stress.* Delacorte Press, New York.

Bohm, David (1980): *Wholeness and the Implicate Order.* Routledge and Kegan Paul, London.

Bolen, Jean Shinoda (2004): *The Tao of Psychology: Synchronicity and the Self.* HarperCollins Publishers, New York.

Brenneis, Sandra and Frederic Boersma (1993): "Typology and Trance: Developing Synchronicity in Hypnotic Induction" in *Medical Hypnoanalysis Journal* 8, no. 2, pp. 45–56.

Brown, Georg S. (1957): *Probability and Scientific Inference.* Longmans, London.

Burniston, Andrew F. (1994): "Synchronicity: A Dionysian Perspective," in *Harvest,* Volume 40, pp. 118–27.

Cambray, Joseph (2009): *Synchronicity, Nature and Psyche in an interconnected Universe*. A&M University Press, Texas.

Capra, Fritjof (1975): *The Tao of Physics: An Exploration of the Parallels between Modern Physics and Eastern Mysticism.* Wildwood House, London.

Combs, Allan and Mark Holland (1990): *Synchronicity: Science, Myth, and the Trickster.* Paragon House, New York.

Conklin, Beth A. (2001): *Consuming Grief: Compassionate Cannibalism in an Amazonian Society.* University of Texas Press, Austin.

Cowan, Philip A. (1978): *Piaget with Feeling: Cognitive, Social and Emotional Dimensions.* Holt, Rinehart And Winston, New York.

Diaconis, Persi and Frederick Mosteller (1989): "Methods for Studying Coincidences" in *Journal of the American Statistical Association* 84, no. 408, pp. 853–61.

Dietrich, Wolfgang (2008): *Variationen über die vielen Frieden. Band 1: Deutungen.* VS Verlag für Sozialwissenschaften. Wiesbaden.

- (2011): *Variationen über die vielen Frieden. Band 2: Elicitive Konflikttransformation und die transrationale Wende der Friedenspolitik.* VS Verlag für Sozialwissenschaften. Wiesbaden.
- (2012): *Interpretations of Peace in History and Culture. Many Peaces Volume 1.* Palgrave Macmillan, London.
- (2014): "A Brief Introduction to Transrational Peace Research and Elicitive Conflict Transformation", in *Journal of Conflictology,* Volume 5, Issue 2 (2014). http://journal-of- conflictology.uoc.edu
- (2015): *Variationen über die vielen Frieden. Band 3: Elicitive Conflict Mapping.* VS Verlag für Sozialwissenschaften. Wiesbaden.

Drobisch, Amos (2009): “Das EPR – Gedankenexperiment, die Bellsche Ungleichung und der experimentelle Nachweis von Quantenkorrelationen” Schriftliche Hausarbeit im Rahmen der Ersten Staatsprüfung, dem Landesprüfungsamt für Erste Staatsprüfungen für Lehrämter an Schulen. Institut für Theoretische Physik A Lehr- und Forschungsgebiet Laserphysik. Aachen. Http://llp.ilt.fhg.de/skripten/hausarbeit_drobisch.pdf. Accessed 24/04/2015.

Eckhart, Meister (1980): *Breakthrough.* Trans. M. Fox. Image, New York.

Eliade, Mircea (1964): *Shamanism: Archaic Techniques of Ecstasy.* Trans. Willard R. Trask. Princeton University Press, Princeton.

- (1977): *Yoga: Unsterblichkeit und Freiheit.* Trans. Inge Köck. Insel Verlag, Frankfurt am Main.
- (1982): *A History of Religious Ideas: From Gautama Buddha to the Triumh of Christianity.* Volume 2. Trans. Willard R. Trask. University of Chicago Press, Chicago.

Eriksen, Thomas Hylland (2007): *Små Steder - Store Spørgsmål: Innføring I Sosialantropologi.* Universitetsforlaget Oslo, Oslo.

Etymologisches Wörterbuch des Deutschen (1993): (first published 1989) Akademie Verlag, Berlin

Fienup-Riordan, Ann (1994): “Original Ecologists?: The relationship Between Yup´ik Eskimos and Animals.” In *Eskimo Essays.* Rutgers University Press, New Brunswick, New Jersey.

Fischer, Theo (2005): *Wu wei: Die Lebenskunst des Tao.* Rororo Verlag, Reinbeck.

Fordham, Michael (1957): “Reflections on the Archetypes and Synchronicity” in *New Developments in Analytical Psychology.* Routledge and Kegan Paul, London, pp. 35–50.

Fordham, Michael (1962): “An Interpretation of Jung’s Thesis about Synchronicity,” in *British Journal of Medical Psychology* 35 (1962) 205 – 10

Franz, Marie-Louise von (1974): *Number and Time: Reflections leading towards a Unification of Psychology and Physics.* Northwestern University Press. Rider & Company, London.

- (1975): *C. G. Jung: His Myth in Our Time.* Trans. William H. Kennedy. Hodder and Stoughton, London.
- (1980): *On Divination and Synchronicity : The Psychology of Meaningful Chance: Studies in Jungian Psychology.* Inner City Books, Toronto.
- (1980b): *Projection and Re-Collection in Jungian Psychology: Reflect ions of the Soul.* Trans. William H. Kennedy. Open Court, Lasalle.
- (1980c): *Alchemy: An Introduction to the Symbolism and the Psychology.* Inner City Books, Toronto.

Frazer, Sir James George [1889]: *The Golden Bough: A Study in Magic and Religion.* Oxford´s World Classic Paperbacks (1994). Oxford University Press, New York.

Frey-Wehrlin, C. T. (1976): “Reflections on C. G. Jung´s Concept of Synchronicity” in *Journal of Analytical Psychology,* Volume 21 Issue 1, pp. 37 – 49.

Fried, Wilson, MacDonald and Behnke (1998): “Electric current stimulates laughter” in *Nature* 391, 650.

Gammon, Mary (1973): “‘Window into Eternity’: Archetype and Relativity” in *Journal of Analytical Psychology* 18, no. 1, pp. 11–24.

Garbe, Richard (2013): *Die Samkhya-Philosophie.* Ed. Kar-Maria Gruth. Hofenberg, Berlin. [First published 1894]

Gardner, Howard (1972): *The Quest for Mind.* Vintage, New York.

Gebser, Jean (1973): *Ursprung und Gegenwart. 1. Teil. Die Fundamente der a-perspektivischen Welt.* Deutcher Taschenbuch Verlag. München.

Giegerich, Wolfgang (2012) “A serious misunderstanding: Synchronicity and the generation of meaning”, in *Journal of Analytical Psychology*, 2012, 57, 500–11.

Goethe, Johann Wolfgang (1994): *Faust. Eine Tragödie.* Texte. Hrsg. Edited and published by Albrecht Schöne. Deutscher Klassiker Verlag, Frankfurt am Main. [First published 1808]

Habermas, Jürgen (1979): *Communication and the Evolution of Society.* Beacon Press, Boston.
Hillman, James (1972): "An Essay on Pan," in *Pan and the Nightmare*, by W. H. Roscher and James Hillman. Spring Publications, Zürich, pp. lvi–lix.
Hofmann, Liane and Christian Roesler (2010): "Der Archetyp des verwundeten Heilers" in *Transpersonale Psychologie und Psychotherapie.* 16. Jahrgang, Heft 1, 2010. Via Nova, Petersberg, pp. 75-90.
Huxley, Aldous (1945): *The Perennial Philosophy.* Harper & Brothers, New York.
Inglis, Brian (1990): *Coincidence: A Matter of Chance—or Synchronicity?* Hutchinson, London.
Jacobi, Jolande (1978): *Die Psychologie von C. G. Jung: eine Einführung in das Gesamtwerk.* Fischer Taschenbuch Verlag, Frankfurt a.M. Original from University of Michigan.
Jaffé, Aniela (1978): "Synchronistic Phenomena," in *Apparitions: An Archetypal Approach to Death, Dreams and Ghosts.* Spring, Irving, pp. 187–206.
Jung, C. G. (1950): "Foreword to the 'I Ching'", in *Collected Works*, vol. 11, *Psychology and Religion: West and East*, 2nd ed. (London: Routledge and Kegan Paul, 1969), 589–608.
- (1952): *Bewusstes und Unbewusstes.* Fischer Taschenbuch Verlag, Frankfurt am Main.
- (1964): *Man and his Symbols.* Anchor Press, New York.
- (1966): *Two Essays on Analytical Psychology.* In *Collected Works,* Volume 7. Trans. R. F. C. Hull. Princeton University Press, Princeton.
- (1969): *The Structure and Dynamic of the Psyche.* In *Collected Works,* Vol. 8. Trans. R. F. C. Hull. Princeton University Press, Princeton.
- (1971): *Psychological Types.* In *Collected Works,* Volume 6. Trans. H. G. Baynes. Princeton University Press, Princeton.
- (1978): *Aion* In *Collected Works,* Volume 9, pt. 2. Trans. R. F. C. Hull. Princeton University Press, Princeton.
- (1979): *Mysterium Coniunctionis.* In *Collected Works,* Volume 14. Trans. R. F. C. Hull. Princeton University Press, Princeton.
- (1989a): *Memories, Dreams, Reflections.* (Rev. ed., C. Winston & R. Winston, Trans.) (A. Jaffe, Ed.). Random House, New York.
- (1990): "Synchronizität als ein Prinzip akausaler Zusammenhänge", in *C. G. Jung, Synchronizität, Akausalität und Okkultismus.* Deutscher Taschenbuch Verlag, München. [First published 1952]
- (1990b): *Psychology and Religion West and East.* In *Collected Works,* Volume 11. Trans. R. F. C. Hull. Princeton University Press, Princeton.
Kerenyi, Karl (1976): *Hermes, Guide of Souls: The mythologem of the masculine source of life.* Spring, Dallas.
Keutzer, Caroline S. (1984): "The Power of Meaning: From Quantum Mechanics to Synchronicity" in *Journal of Humanistic Psychology* 24, no. 1, pp. 80–94.
Keutzer, Caroline S. (1982): "Archetypes, Synchronicity and the theory of Formative Causation" in *Journal of Analytical Psychology,* Volume 27, pp. 255-262.
Koestler, Arthur (1967): *The Ghost in the Machine.* Macmillan, New York.
Koestler, Arthur (1972): *The Roots of Coincidence.* Pan Books Ltd, London.
Kämper, Angela (2005): *Tierboten: Was uns Begegnungen mit Tieren sagen.* Wilhelm Goldmann Verlag, München.
Laszlo, Ervin (2000): *Das fünfte Feld.* Bastei Lübbe Verlag, Köln.
Levy-Bruhl, Lucien (1923): *Primitive Mentality.* Macmillan Company, New York.
Main, Roderick (2007): *Revelations of Chance: Synchronicity as Spiritual Experience.* State University of New York Press, Albany.
Mansfield, Victor (1995): *Synchronicity, Science, and Soul Making.* Open Court Publishing, Chicago.
Martin Buber (1953): *Gottesfinsternis. Betrachtungen zur Beziehung zwischen Religion und Philosophie.* Manesse Verlag, Zürich.

McDermott, Robert A. (1993): "Transpersonal Worldviews: Historical and Philosophical Reflections" in *Paths Beyond Ego: The Transpersonal Vision.* Jeremy P. Tarcher/Perigee Books, Los Angeles.
McLeod, S. A. (2009): *Jean Piaget.* Retrieved from http://www.simplypsychology.org/piaget.html
Meinhold, Werner J. (1997): *Das große Handbuch der Hypnose: Theorie und Praxis der Fremd- und Selbsthypnose.* Ariston Verlag, München.
Mill, J. S. (1869): *On Liberty.* The Walter Scott Publishing Co., Ltd. London.
Mindell, Arnold (1975): "The Golem: An Image Governing Synchronicity" in *Quadrant* 8, no. 2, pp. 5–16.
Mungello, David E. (1999): "How Central to Leibniz's Philosophy was China?" In: *Das Neueste über China. G. W. Leibnizens Novissima Sinica von 1697.* Hrsg. von Wenchao Li und Hans Poser. Franz Steiner Verlag, Stuttgart.
Neumann, Erich (1949): *Ursprungsgeschichte des Bewusstseins.* Buchdruckerei Winterthur AG., Winterthur.
- (1955): "Narzissmus, Automorphismus und Urbeziehung" in *Studien zur Analytischen Psychologie C. G. Jungs I.* Rascher, Zürich.
- (1956): "The Psyche and the Transformation of the Reality Planes." Trans. Hildegard Nagel. In *Spring,* pp. 81 – 111.
Peat, F. David (1989): *Synchronizität.* Scherz Verlag, München.
Pfeifer, Wolfgang (1997): *Etymologisches Wörterbuch des Deutschen.*Deutscher Taschenbuch Verlag.
Piaget, Jean (1972): *Sprechen und Denken des Kindes.* Schwann Verlag, Düsseldorf.
Piaget, Jean (1977): *The essential Piaget.* Edited by Howard E. Gruber and J. Jacques Voneche. Basic Books, New York.
Progoff, Ira (1973): *Jung, Synchronicity, and Human Destiny: Noncausal Dimensions of Human Experience.* Delta Books, New York.
Rhine, J. B. (1956): *The Reach of the Mind.* Faber and Faber, London.
Risi, Armin (2007): *Gott und die Götter: Das Mysteriumwissen der vedischen Hochkultur.* Govinda Verlag, Budapest.
Robertson, Robin (2002): "Synchronicity in a New Light" in *Psychological Perspectives: A Quarterly Journal of Jungian Thought,* Volume 43 Issue 1, pp. 92-109.
Schopenhauer, Arthur (1922): *Transscendente Spekulation über die anscheinende Absichtlichkeit im Schicksale des Einzelnen.* In *Schopenhauers sämmtliche Schriften in fünf Bänden.* Volume 4. ed. E. Grisebach.[First published 1851]
Shanks, Lewis Piaget (1924): "Henri-Frederic Amiel, 1821-1881." in *The Open Court: A Monthly Magazin.*Vol. XXXV (No. 11), Open Court Publishing Company, pp. 641 – 657.
Sheldrake, Rupert (1981): *A New Science of Life: The Hypothesis of Formative Causation.* Blond and Briggs, London.
Sheldrake, Rupert (1988): *The Presence of the Past.* Collins, London.
Stuckrad, Kocku von (2004): *Was ist Esoterik?* Beck, München.
Surprise, Kirby (2012): *Synchronicity: The Art of Coincidence, Choice, and Unlocking your Mind.* Career Press, Pompton Plains, NJ.
The Bible. New Internation Version. Biblica.
Tränkle, Hermann (1985): „Gnothi seauton. Zu Ursprung und Deutungsgeschichte des delphischen Spruchs" in *Würzburger Jahrbücher für die Altertumswissenschaft.* Neue Folge, Bd. 11, 1985.
Uyldert, Mellie (1990): *Kosmische Zusammenhänge: Grundlagen der Astrologie* Trans. Clemens Wilhelm. Hugendubel, München.
Vaughn, Frances and Roger Walsh (1993): "Problems on the Path: Clinical Concerns" in *Paths Beyond Ego: The Transpersonal Vision.* Jeremy P. Tarcher/Perigee Books, Los Angeles.
Walsh, Roger (1993): "Mapping and Comparing States" in *Paths Beyond Ego: The Transpersonal Vision.* Jeremy P. Tarcher/Perigee Books, Los Angeles.

Watt, Caroline (1991): "Psychology and Coincidences" in *European Journal of Parapsychology 8*, pp. 73- 74.
Webster's Comprehensive Dictionary (2004): Encyclopedic Edition, Typhoon International.
Wilber, Ken (1993): "The Pre/Trans Fallacy" in *Paths Beyond Ego: The Transpersonal Vision.* Jeremy P. Tarcher/Perigee Books, Los Angeles.
Wilber, Ken (2000): *Sex, Ecology, &Spirituality: The Spirit of Evolution.* Shambhala Press, Boston.
William, James [1902]: *The Varieties of Religious Experience: A Study in Human Nature. Being the Gifford Lectures on Natural Religion Delivered at Edingburgh in 1901–1902.* (paperback), Classics, Library of America, 2010.
Williams, Mary (1957): "An Example of Synchronicity" in *Journal of Analytical Psychology* 2, no. 1, pp. 93–95.
Wittgenstein, Ludwig (1955): *Tractatus logico-philosophicus.* Routledge & Paul Kegan, London. [First Published 1921]

MIX
Papier aus verantwortungsvollen Quellen
Paper from responsible sources
FSC® C105338

If you have any concerns about our products,
you can contact us on
ProductSafety@springernature.com

In case Publisher is established outside the EU,
the EU authorized representative is:
Springer Nature Customer Service Center GmbH
Europaplatz 3, 69115 Heidelberg, Germany

Printed by Libri Plureos GmbH
in Hamburg, Germany